very easy
Circular Knits

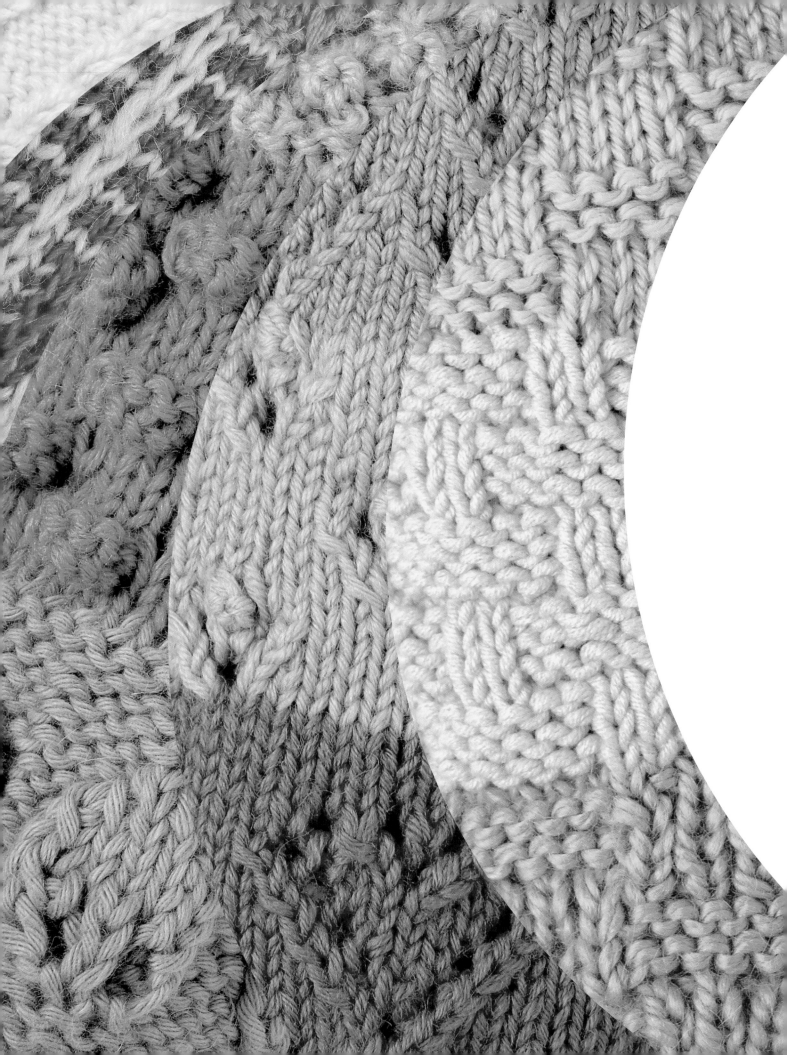

very easy
Circular Knits

Simple techniques and step-by-step projects
for the well-rounded knitter

Betty Barnden

C&T PUBLISHING

A Quarto Book

First published in 2007 by
C&T Publishing Inc
1651 Challenge Drive
Concord
CA 94520–5206
www.ctpub.com

ISBN-10: 1–57120–427–X
ISBN-13: 978–1–57120–427–1

Conceived, designed, and published by
Quarto Publishing plc
The Old Brewery
6 Blundell Street
London N7 9BH

QUAR.ECK

Senior Editor Liz Pasfield
Art Editor Julie Joubinaux
Designer Julie Francis
Assistant Art Director Penny Cobb
Pattern Checkers Eva Yates, Claire Rowan
Copy Editor Sarah Hoggett
Photographers Phil Wilkins, Andrew Atkinson
Stylist Lone Sigurdsson
Illustrator Kate Simunek

Art Director Moira Clinch
Publisher Paul Carslake

Manufactured by Pica Digital Ltd, Singapore
Printed in Singapore

9 8 7 6 5 4 3 2 1

Contents

Introduction

The craft of circular knitting is thought to be more than a thousand years old. Some of the earliest known examples of knitting were made "in the round." Fragments of tubular socks (some with divided toes, for thong sandals), found in Egypt, have been dated to about the eleventh century A.D., although knitting may have existed long before that. Due to the fragile nature of knitted fabrics, nobody really knows.

It may seem strange, but it is now thought possible that circular knitting developed before, rather than after, the row-by-row knitting of flat pieces. Just consider: cloth for garments such as shirts and cloaks could easily be woven in flat pieces on a loom, then cut and stitched to shape. But making satisfactory socks, that cling to the foot and are constructed without uncomfortable seams, requires knitting (or a similar technique, such as crochet) worked "in the round," to make a flexible tube with no seams. So there was no real need for flat knitting, but the tubular, fitted sock was a marvelous invention!

Through the centuries, circular knitting developed into a complex craft: shapings for caps and purses, and for the heels and toes of socks, have taken many forms across the world. Decorative textured stitches, and patterns in two or more colors, were devised and passed down from one generation to the next. Being warm, light, and comfortable, knitting was used to make all kinds of practical garments. In addition, knitted hats and other woolen articles were often felted (by boiling and shrinking) to make them weatherproof. In sixteenth-century Europe, the manufacture of fine steel needles made intricate knitting feasible, and silk stockings made in Spain were highly prized. From the Shetland Islands to South America, local knitting traditions provide a whole world of patterns and techniques for us to study.

As the range of knitted garments grew to include larger articles such as jackets and sweaters, hand-knitting in flat pieces became more popular, perhaps due to the difficulty of controlling large numbers of stitches on double-pointed needles. However, the invention of the circular knitting needle in the early twentieth century made it much easier to knit larger garments. Modern circular needles with plastic cords are light, smooth, and practically unbreakable, so large projects can now be tackled with ease, and this has inspired a revival of circular knitting.

Circular knitting is fascinating; to me, it is the most satisfying kind of knitting. A garment knitted "in the round," without seams, has no weak points to come apart and is flexible and comfortable to wear. With a few balls of yarn and a circular needle (or a set of double-pointed needles), you can construct a flexible, three-dimensional tubular shape that takes exactly the form you want. Traditional methods for shaping heels, toes, thumbs, fingers, sweater yokes, and hats can be adapted to make up-to-date garments and accessories in modern yarns.

By learning the traditional techniques of circular knitting, and at the same time exploring the wide range of beautiful yarns available today, we can create our own twenty-first–century version of this ancient craft.

Happy knitting!

Materials and equipment

Yarns, special needles, and a few accessories are all you need to start circular knitting. Many different yarns are available today, so this section starts with a brief guide to the different terms used to describe them, to help you purchase the right type and amount for each project. If you are already a knitter, you will probably own most of the equipment that you need for circular knitting, with the possible exception of the needles.

Yarns

There's a bewildering variety of yarns available today from specialist yarn stores and websites. Descriptions of yarn weights and types differ from one manufacturer to another, and from one country to another, but here's a rough guide to help you find what you want.

Yarn weights

There are many different weights, or thicknesses, of yarn, and the jargon can be confusing: one manufacturer's aran-weight, for example, may be somewhat finer or heavier than another's. The examples here are plain wool and cotton yarns, shown actual size, to help you understand the different terms used. See page 17 for suitable needle sizes.

Fine yarn that is described as 2-ply, 3-ply, or lace-weight (and sometimes as sock weight) is used to make delicate articles, and for fine, close knitting on small needles.

4-ply, or fingering, yarn is a fine-to-medium weight yarn suitable for socks, gloves, and baby wear.

Sport and double-knitting yarns are medium-weight yarns with a wide range of uses. These popular weights are available in a huge choice of colors and fibers.

Aran-weight and worsted yarns are a little heavier than sport and double-knitting yarns. They are suitable for many garments and accessories, and again are available in a wide range of colors and fibers.

Bulky and chunky yarns are great for quick-to-knit projects on large needles. Many of the new fancy yarns being developed today fall into this category, which has more variation than any other: some extra-thick yarns are described as extra bulky, or super chunky.

TIPS

- When buying more than one ball of the same color, make sure that the dye lot numbers match, otherwise the slight difference in color may spoil your project.
- When substituting yarn for that quoted in any knitting instructions, choose a yarn with the same recommended gauge as the instructions. (If you can, buy a single ball and test your own gauge using the method described on page 42.) If the instructions quote the yardage, match this, too, if possible—or use the quoted yardage to calculate how many balls of yarn you will need.

Ball band information

The information given on the ball band of any yarn can help you decide whether that yarn is suitable for your project.

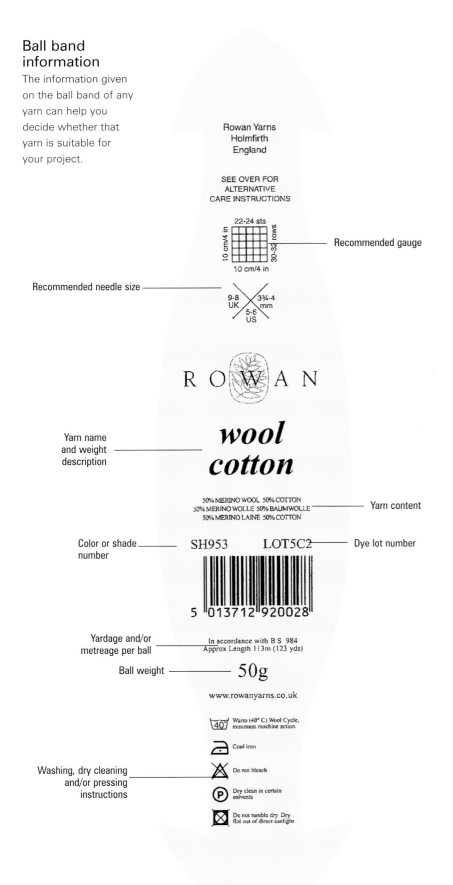

Rowan Yarns
Holmfirth
England

SEE OVER FOR
ALTERNATIVE
CARE INSTRUCTIONS

Recommended gauge

Recommended needle size

ROWAN

wool cotton

50% MERINO WOOL 50% COTTON
50% MERINO WOLLE 50% BAUMWOLLE
50% MERINO LAINE 50% COTTON — Yarn content

Yarn name and weight description

Color or shade number — SH953 LOT5C2 — Dye lot number

5 013712 920028

Yardage and/or metreage per ball — In accordance with B S 984
Approx Length 113m (123 yds)

Ball weight — 50g

www.rowanyarns.co.uk

Washing, dry cleaning and/or pressing instructions

40° — Warm (40° C) Wool Cycle, minimum machine action

Cool iron

Do not bleach

P — Dry clean in certain solvents

Do not tumble dry Dry flat out of direct sunlight

Yarn fibers

Yarns may be manufactured from any of the following fiber types, either as single-fiber yarns, or in blends of two or three fibers together:

Wool and other animal fibers: Wool from sheep, mohair from goats, angora from rabbits, alpaca, camelhair, and many other animal fibers may be spun into yarn that is usually warm and soft. Wool, in particular, makes an elastic yarn that will return to shape after stretching.

Cotton and other vegetable fibers: Cotton from the cotton plant, linen from flax, hemp, ramie, and bamboo are just some of the plant fibers used today to make knitting yarns. In general, these yarns are cool and smooth to the touch, with less elasticity than wool.

Silk: Silk threads are obtained from the cocoon of the silkworm, and are used in different qualities from smooth and fine through to coarse and uneven. Pure silk yarn is cool to the touch with a subtle sheen, and rather expensive, so silk is often blended with other fibers such as cotton.

Synthetic yarns: Synthetic yarns are derived from coal or petroleum products and spun to resemble natural fibers. These fibers have improved considerably over the last few years. They are relatively cheap, hard wearing, and often machine washable. They are often blended with natural fibers to produce yarns that combine the best qualities of both fiber types.

Viscose rayon: This fiber is man-made but, being derived from cellulose (from timber), it is not strictly a "synthetic" product. Viscose rayon fiber is smooth and glossy. It is often blended with matt fibers, such as wool or cotton, to make interesting fancy yarns.

Yarn types

Yarns can be constructed in many ways to provide different effects when knitted. Some yarn types, such as tweeds, are old favorites, while new types are being developed all the time. Look out for anything unusual. It's always fun to try out novelty yarns, alone or in combination with plain yarns. Here are some of the types you may find:

Tweed yarns

Traditional tweed yarns contain flecks and strands of several colors together, giving a soft, blurry effect.

Lopi or soft-spun yarns

Lopi yarn, originally made in Iceland, is a warm, thick wool yarn that is hardly twisted at all, making it soft and thick but relatively light to wear.

Slub yarns

Many fiber types may be spun as slub yarns, meaning that the thickness varies between thick and thin, which adds an interesting texture to the knitting.

Bouclé yarns

Bouclé yarn is made by twisting two yarns together, one at a looser tension than the other. The looser yarn forms little curls or twists.

Fluffy and fuzzy yarns

Mohair and angora fibers make naturally fluffy yarns. Other fuzzy effects are obtained by special spinning techniques: chenille yarn, for example, is made by trapping short fibers across a tightly spun core; eyelash yarns trap longer, silkier fibers in a similar way.

Metallic yarns

Metallic yarns (sometimes called lurex yarns) add sparkle to your work. Some types, such as the frizzy gold thread shown here, are designed to be wound and knitted together with another, plainer yarn.

Tape and ladder yarns

These yarns are flat in profile, like a narrow ribbon, or sometimes a flattened tube. Knitted in simple stitches, they tend to produce a loose, elastic fabric.

Multi-color yarns

Yarns may be dip-dyed or spray-dyed with several different colors. Such yarns are sometimes described as "random-dyed," "shaded," or "instant fairisle." The effect when knitted depends on the length of yarn between color changes: long lengths of colors make stripes or streaks across the knitting, while shorter lengths of colors give a more spotted or patchy effect.

Needles

In circular knitting, the stitches are worked in a circle to form a seamless tube (unlike flat knitting, which is worked back and forth in rows). To work circular knitting, you need either a circular needle, or a set of double-pointed needles. To find out how to choose the correct needles for your project, turn to pages 16–17.

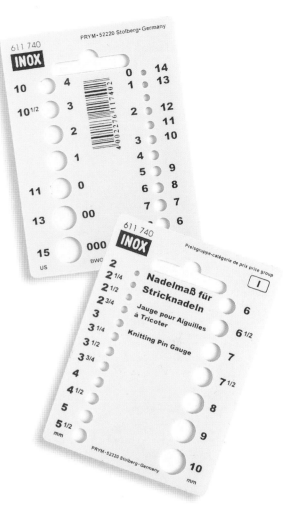

Double-pointed needles

These are supplied in sets of four or five, in the usual range of sizes (see page 17) and various lengths from 4 in. (10 cm) to 16 in. (40 cm). They may be made of metal, plastic, wood, or bamboo.

Circular needles

These have two rigid tips of metal, plastic, wood, or bamboo, joined by a flexible length of plastic cord. The usual range of sizes is available (see page 17), in a range of lengths from 12 in. (30 cm) to 100 in. (250 cm) or more.

Interchangeable needle kit

This useful kit includes ten pairs of rigid, plastic needle tips and six flexible cords of different lengths, plus extender pieces (to join two lengths of cord) and end-stops (for putting work aside, or using the tips and cords for flat knitting). Such kits are quite expensive, but may be a sound investment if circular knitting becomes your favorite craft.

Needle gauge

Some modern needles have the size printed on them, but others are not marked, and a needle gauge is very useful for checking sizes. The holes on this gauge are marked on one side with US sizes and British Wire Gauge sizes, and on the other side with European sizes in millimeters. The British Wire Gauge (BWG) sizing system is no longer in use, but if you have a stash of old needles or vintage knitting patterns, a gauge like this is invaluable.

> **TIPS**
>
> - Thrift stores can be a good source for building up a collection of any type of knitting needle—but you will need a needle gauge to check the sizes!
> - Sets of double-pointed needles that have lost their packaging may be bundled together for storage. Pony-tail bands last longer than ordinary elastic bands.
> - Always store needles flat in a box or drawer, never standing on their tips in a jar or pot.

Essential extras

In addition to your collection of needles, you will need various other accessories to complete any project. Keep the following items in your workbag.

Scissors

You will also need a small pair of scissors to cut the yarn. Never break yarn between your fingers.

Tapestry needles

A tapestry needle has a large eye to take yarn easily, and a blunt tip so that it will slip between the knitted stitches without splitting the yarn. Sometimes tapestry needles are sold as "knitters' needles." Different sizes are available to suit different weights of yarn.

Darning needle

Sometimes you need a needle with a sharp point, such as a darning needle with a large eye.

Pins

Although there are very few seams in circular knitting, you will need a few pins to check your gauge correctly (see page 42). Choose pins with large heads that will not disappear between the knitted stitches.

Tape measure

You will need a tape measure to check your gauge (see page 42) and to measure work in progress (see page 43).

Stitch holders

These are used to leave aside a group of stitches while work continues on the remainder. Several types are available; for small groups of stitches, you can substitute a large safety pin (see page 53).

Ring markers

Although ring markers are not strictly essential, they are a very useful addition to your workbag. A ring marker, placed on the needle and slipped from round to round, makes it easy to count completed rounds, or to place shapings correctly without counting the stitches every time, (see page 31).

Other accessories

In addition to the essential equipment, there are a few other items you may find useful. These may be acquired as the need arises.

Split markers

Split markers are designed to hook onto a particular knitted stitch, to mark a position from which stitches or rounds may later be counted (see page 31).

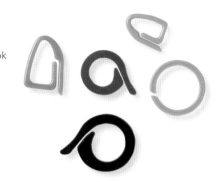

Bobbins

Small amounts of yarn for colored pattern work (see pages 82 and 120–124) may be wound onto bobbins to prevent tangling.

Cable needles

These are used when working cable stitch patterns (see pages 72 and 112–113). They may be straight, cranked, or curved, choose whichever you find works best for you.

Round counter

This type of row counter is activated by simply pressing the top every time you complete a round. (The usual type of row counter, or row tally, which slips onto the end of a straight knitting needle with a knob, is not suitable for use on either a circular needle or on double-pointed needles.)

Point protectors

Various sizes and designs of little plastic caps are available to protect the points of your needles when you put work aside.

chapter one
Circular Knitting Know-how

If you have never knitted on a circular needle, follow the guidelines in this chapter. Many of the techniques shown are almost the same as for flat knitting on two needles, but with a few twists that you need to understand. Other techniques are specific to circular knitting.

All the basic skills, from holding the yarn and needles, through casting on, knitting, purling, binding off, increasing, decreasing, assembly, and checking your gauge, are shown on a circular needle. Knitting on a set of double-pointed needles can seem confusing at first, but where the method differs from that used for circular needle knitting, we've put the information in a separate panel for you.

Choosing needles

For circular knitting, you need either a circular needle or a set of double-pointed needles (see page 11). As a general rule, circular needles are used to knit tubes larger than 16 in. (40 cm) in circumference, while double-pointed needles may be used for tubes of any size.

Circular needle tips and double-pointed needles may be made of plastic, metal, wood, or bamboo. Metal is often used for the smallest sizes (for strength), and plastic for the largest (for lightness in weight). Some people prefer plastic, for its lighter weight; others like the feel of wooden needles, which can be useful for controlling slippery yarns such as viscose. Try different types to find out which you prefer.

Circular needles

A circular needle consists of two rigid tips about 4–6 in. (10–15 cm) in length, joined by a flexible cord. The tips may be plastic, metal, wood, or bamboo; nowadays, the cord is usually plastic or nylon. The joins between the cord and tips should be perfectly smooth to avoid snagging the stitches.

The size of the needle is determined by the diameter of the solid tips, and the sizes of circular needles match the sizes of single-pointed pairs of needles (see table, opposite).

The length of the needle is measured from point to point and ranges from 12 in. (30 cm) through 16 in. (40 cm), 20 in. (50 cm), and so on up to 100 in. (250 cm) or more. It is most important to choose a needle that is at least 4 in. (10 cm) shorter than the circumference of the knitting, so that the stitches will not be stretched around the needle. In fact, a circular needle can accommodate the stitches for a tube up to about four times larger than the needle. A 16-in. (40-cm) length, for example, will suit a knitted tube between 20 and 64 in. (50 and 160 cm) in circumference.

Wrong!
This circular needle is too long for the number of stitches. Stitches will be difficult (or impossible) to work, and the resulting knitting will be stretched out of shape.

Right!
When the same number of stitches is arranged on a shorter circular needle they are comfortably bunched together, making them easy to work into.

Double-pointed needles

Double-pointed needles have a point at each end, and may be made from plastic, metal, wood, or bamboo. Sets may consist of four or five needles.

Double-pointed needles are most often used for knitting small tubes. They are more adaptable than circular needles, because the length you choose is not so critical: even tiny tubes, such as fingers for gloves, can be knitted on long double-pointed needles.

The size of a double-pointed needle is determined by the diameter, in the same way as single-pointed and circular needles (see table below).

The length of the needles can vary from 4 in. (10 cm) up to 16 in. (40 cm) or more. When knitting, the stitches are arranged on three needles (from a set of four), or on four needles (from a set of five), with the last needle being used to work the stitches (see pages 24–25). So you must choose a needle that can easily hold one third (or one quarter) of the stitches without bunching up, otherwise the stitches may fall off the points. In fact, you can use quite long needles to knit small tubes; just push each set of stitches to the center of the needle. For a large project, you can put two or more sets of needles together to suit any number of stitches, although a circular needle is easier to handle.

Wrong!
These needles are too short. As you knit, the stitches will tend to drop off the points.

Right!
When the same number of stitches is arranged on longer needles, they are safely positioned at the center of each needle.

Needle sizes

Needles are sized in the US from 0 to about 20, and in Europe from 2 mm to 15 mm or more. The two systems do not match exactly, but if you always check your gauge (see page 42) you can use needles from either system, as available.

US	EUROPE	APPROX. YARN TYPE
0	2 mm	2-ply/lace fingering
1	2.25 mm	3-ply/sock weight
2	3 mm	4-ply/fingering
3	3.25 mm	4-ply/fingering/sport
4	3.5 mm	sport
5	3.75 mm	double knitting/sport
6	4 mm	double knitting/sport
7	4.5 mm	worsted
8	5 mm	worsted/Aran
9	5.5 mm	Aran/chunky/bulky
10	6 mm	chunky/bulky
10.5	6.5 or 7 mm	chunky/bulky
11	8 mm	super chunky/extra bulky
13	9 mm	super chunky/extra bulky
15	10 mm	super chunky/extra bulky
17	12 or 13 mm	specialist yarn weights
20	15 mm	specialist yarn weights

TIPS

- Most circular needles are supplied in plastic pockets. The sizes are rarely marked on the needles themselves, so always store them in their original pockets. The cord should be smoothly rolled, not kinked.
- If a circular needle cord does become kinked, soak the needle in a bowl of hand-hot water for a few minutes, and then gently stretch it between your fingers to straighten it out.
- Store double-pointed needles in their original plastic pockets, too, or bundle each set together with a rubber band.
- Keep a needle gauge in your work bag and always check the size of any unmarked needle before you use it.

Holding yarn

To keep the yarn at an even tension as you knit, you need to twist it loosely around your fingers as you pick up the needle(s). If you hold the yarn too loosely, your stitches will be loose and uneven. If you hold it too tightly, your stitches will also be tight, and therefore difficult to work. There are several ways to hold the yarn, but this method is the most usual.

In your right hand

For the Scottish (or English) method of knitting (see page 19), hold the yarn in your right hand.

1 Wind the yarn around your right little finger
Scoop up the yarn with your little finger, as shown, about 6 in. (15 cm) from the needle tip.

2 Wind the yarn around your right forefinger
Turn your hand so that the palm faces downward and slide your forefinger under the yarn, close to the needle tip. The yarn is wound once around your little finger.

In your left hand

For the German (or Continental) method of knitting (see page 19), hold the yarn in your left hand.

1 Wind the yarn around your left fingers
Wind the yarn around the fingers of your left hand, as shown.

Holding needles

There are several ways to hold knitting needles, whether circular, straight, or double-pointed (see box, right). These two methods both work well for circular knitting, so try them out to see which works for you.

Holding double-pointed needles

When you are working on double-pointed needles, the two needles in use may be held by either the Scottish (English) or the German (Continental) method.

Scottish or English method

This method of holding the needles provides a good grip for a set of double-pointed needles. Hold the empty needle in your right hand and the needle you are working into in your left. The other two needles are held in place by the stitches. As you knit toward the end of each needle, change your left-hand grip to include the tip of the next needle, to avoid stretching the yarn across the gap between the needles.

German or Continental method

This method also works well with double-pointed needles. Hold the empty needle in your right hand and the needle you are working into in your left. The other two needles are held in place by the stitches. Avoid stretching the work, as described above.

Scottish (or English) method

This is the easiest method for a novice knitter. Hold the yarn in your right hand.

1 Hold needle tips and yarn
Pick up the yarn in your right hand, as shown opposite. Hold one end of the circular needle in each hand, quite close to the needle tips, with the rest of the needle beneath your palms. Hold each needle tip in the same way that you would hold a knife.

2 Balance needle tips as you knit
As you knit, you need to relax your grip on the right needle tip, without letting go completely, to carry the yarn forward around the needle tip. Practice keeping the right needle in place by balancing it with your right thumb.

German (or Continental) method

For this method the yarn is held in the left hand and the right-hand needle does most of the work.

1 Hold needle tips and yarn
Pick up the yarn in your left hand, as shown opposite, and hold the needle tips under your palms, like knives.

2 Move right needle to catch yarn
The knitting movement differs from the Scottish or English method. Instead of carrying the yarn around the needle tip, move the right needle tip to scoop up the yarn from right to left, and pull it through to make the stitch, as shown.

Casting on

Before you begin to knit, you need to make a series of linked stitches on the needle, which will not unravel. This is known as casting on. There are several ways to cast on. Some methods make a firm, elastic edge suitable for the lower edge of a garment or cuff, others a looser edge suitable for joining with a seam, or for picking up stitches later (see page 55). Three useful cast-ons are shown here.

All methods of casting on begin with a slipknot.

Making a slipknot

This method makes a slipknot that sits neatly on the needle and may be tightened to match the cast-on stitches that follow.

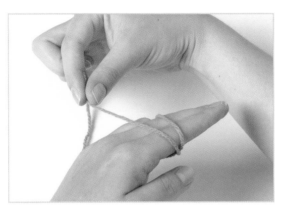

1 Loop the yarn twice
Loop the yarn twice around two fingers of your left hand, making the first turn halfway along your fingers and the second turn closer to the base of your fingers.

2 Draw a loop through
Use the needle tip to draw the second loop through the first and turn the needle to twist the loop as shown.

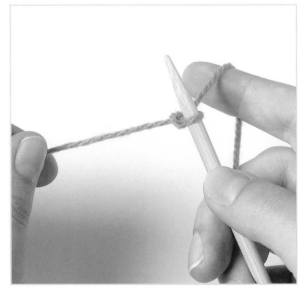

3 Tighten on needle
Release the yarn and pull on the two ends to tighten the knot gently up to the needle. It should not be too tight.

Long-tail cast-on

This method is also known as the German or thumb method. Used to begin circular knitting, it makes a firm, smoothly twisted edge that is quite elastic and suitable for the lower edge of a sweater or cuff, or the top edge of a sock.

1 Make a slipknot with a long tail
Pull out a length of yarn from the ball, about three times the length of the cast-on edge that you are making. Make a slipknot, as shown opposite, and slip it onto the right needle tip, held in your right hand.

2 Hold both ends of yarn
Loop the tail of yarn around your left thumb in the direction shown, and hold the yarn leading to the ball in your right hand as shown on page 18.

3 Catch the yarn through the loop
Slide the needle through the loop on your thumb and catch the yarn leading to the ball around your right forefinger, from right to left.

4 Make the new stitch
Draw the new stitch through, allowing the loop to slip off your thumb and over the needle tip. Catch the yarn tail again with your left thumb and pull gently to tighten the new stitch on the needle. Do not pull too tightly.

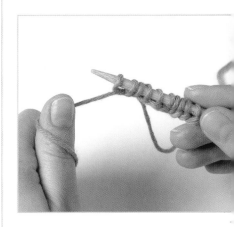

5 Repeat as required
Your thumb is now in the correct position to begin the next stitch. Repeat Steps 3 and 4 as required, pushing the new stitches along the needle away from the tip. They should move easily; if they do not, you have pulled them too tightly. (When you come to knit the first round, the cast-on stitches should be easy to knit.)

Cable cast-on

This is sometimes called the two-needle method. Note how the edge differs in appearance from the long-tail cast-on. This method is also firm and elastic, suitable for the edges of garments.

1 Make a slipknot

Make a slipknot (see page 20) with a tail of yarn at least 4 in. (10 cm) long, which will be run in later. Place it on one needle tip, held in your left hand. This is the first stitch. Hold the yarn and needle tips by your chosen method (see pages 18–19) and insert the right needle tip through the stitch from left to right.

3 Slip to left needle

Pass the left needle tip through the new loop from right to left, and allow the loop to slip off the right needle onto the left. The left needle now holds two stitches.

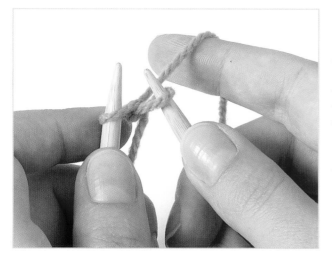

2 Draw a new loop through

For the Scottish or English grip, carry the yarn counterclockwise around the right needle tip. Draw the yarn through, making a new loop on the right needle, as shown. (For the German or Continental grip, use the right needle tip to scoop up the yarn in front of your left forefinger, from right to left. Draw the yarn through, making a new loop on the right needle.)

4 Insert needle between two stitches

Insert the right needle below the left, behind both "legs" of the last stitch you made (not through the stitch, as before). Both "legs" of the last stitch made should be to the right of the inserted needle.

5 Make another new loop

Wrap or catch the yarn and draw it through to make another new loop on the right needle.

Simple thumb cast-on

This cast-on method makes a rather loose edge of single loops. It is often used within the body of the knitting—for example, when constructing a mitten thumb (see pages 58–59). Use this method where stitches are to be picked up at a later stage (see page 55), as it makes a less bulky join than other methods.

1 Wind yarn around thumb

Use your right thumb to scoop up the working yarn from back to front, as shown.

2 Slip loop onto needle

Slide the loop from your thumb onto the right needle tip.

6 Repeat as required

Repeat Steps 3 through 5, pushing the new stitches away from the left needle tip, until you have the required number of stitches on the needle.

3 Repeat

Repeat Steps 1 and 2 as required.

Preparing to knit

Before you begin to knit, you need to arrange the stitches on the needle(s) so that the first cast-on stitch is next to the last cast-on stitch.

Arranging stitches on a circular needle

You must arrange the stitches on a circular needle without twisting them, before you begin to knit. If they are twisted around the needle, the piece of knitting you make will be permanently twisted too.

Wrong!
If the edge is twisted like this, your knitting will be twisted too.

1 Arrange in a circle
Lay the circular needle on a flat surface with the needle tips away from you. The needle tip with the yarn leading to the ball should be on the right. Adjust the position of the stitches so that the cast-on edge is on the inside of the needle, all around.

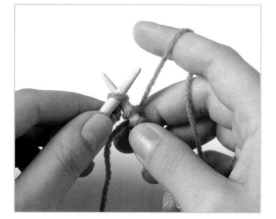

2 Hold yarn and needles
Pick up the work, lifting the two needle tips toward you. The tip with the yarn leading to the ball should be in your right hand. Hold the yarn and needles by your chosen method (see pages 18–19). The yarn leading to the ball should lie loosely to the right, not down through the center of the circle. Now you are ready to knit the first round.

Arranging stitches on double-pointed needles

When you are knitting with a set of double-pointed needles, the cast-on stitches must be arranged on three needles (if you are using a set of four) or on four needles (if you are using a set of five).

1 Cast on onto one needle
Using any of the methods shown on pages 20–23, cast on the number of stitches required onto one needle of the correct size. This needle can be double-pointed, straight, or circular, but it must be long enough to hold all the stitches you require.

2 Insert one double-pointed needle
Hold the needle with the cast-on stitches in your left hand and one double-pointed needle from the set in your right hand. Insert the tip from right to left, through the last stitch that you cast on.

3 Slip first stitch purlwise
Slip the stitch from the left needle to the right. (That is, slip the stitch purlwise, as shown on page 37.)

4 Slip stitches onto three needles
Repeat Steps 2 and 3 until one-third of the stitches are on the right needle. Then slip the next third onto a second double-pointed needle, and the final third onto a third double-pointed needle. Some instructions will tell you exactly how many stitches to arrange on each needle. If the instructions are not specific, then just divide the stitches approximately into thirds.

5 Arrange in a triangle
Arrange the three needles in a triangle, with the yarn leading to the ball at your right as shown. The cast-on edge should be inside the triangle, all around, and not twisted. Push all the stitches on each needle in toward the center of the needle, so that they will not slip off. Note how the leading tip of each needle (reading counterclockwise) overlaps the end of the next needle.

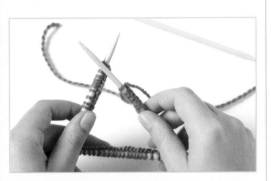

6 Pick up two needles
Pick up the needle tip with the first cast-on stitch in your left hand, and the tip with the last cast-on stitch in your right hand, lifting the needle tips toward you. Allow the other needle and its stitches to rest in your lap, away from your hands. The yarn leading to the ball should lie loosely to your right, not down through the center of the needles.

Arranging stitches on a set of five double-pointed needles
When you are working with a set of five needles, arrange the stitches evenly on four needles in the same way as above, forming a square. Use the fifth needle to begin the first round.

7 Pick up fourth needle
Hold the yarn by your chosen method (see page 18). Hold the needle tip with the first cast-on stitch in your left hand. Pick up the fourth needle of the set in your right hand. Now you are ready to knit the first round.

Working in rounds

You are now ready to work in rounds, with the cast-on edge arranged in a circle.

To knit a round: Scottish (or English) method

Knitting every round produces a tube of stockinette-stitch fabric, with the smooth side on the outside. When you put work aside, push the stitches away from the needle tips, as shown here, so that they are all held on the cord. The stitches are loose around the cord, so the yarn is not stretched, and they will not easily slip up onto the tips and off the needle.

1 Hold the needle tips toward you
Hold the circular needle with the needle tips toward you and the rest of the needle in your lap, away from you. You will knit around the circle from the outside, so the right side of the work is on the outside of the tube of knitting. Slip a ring marker onto the right needle tip to mark the beginning and end of the round.

2 Insert needle and wrap yarn
Insert the right needle tip into the first stitch on the left needle tip, from left to right. Wrap the yarn on your right forefinger counterclockwise around the right needle tip.

3 Make a knit stitch
Draw the new loop toward you, through the stitch, dropping the stitch from the left needle tip. You have one new stitch on the right needle tip.

4 Repeat to end of round
Repeat Steps 2 and 3 until you reach the marker. One round is complete. Slip the marker from the left needle tip to the right, and knit the next round in the same way.

To knit a round: German (or Continental) method

To knit each stitch, insert the right needle as in Step 2 of the Scottish (or English) method, and scoop up the yarn on your left forefinger, from right to left. Draw the new loop through in the same way, as in Step 3 of the Scottish (or English) method.

To purl a round: Scottish (or English) method

A single round of purl stitches makes a ridge on a background of stockinette (in which all rounds are knit). Working entirely in purl rounds makes reverse stockinette stitch (see page 106).

1 Bring yarn to front, insert needle
Mark the beginning of the round with a slip marker on the right needle, as on page 26. Bring the yarn toward you, between the two needle tips. Insert the right needle tip through the first stitch on the left needle from right to left.

2 Wrap yarn
Wrap the yarn counterclockwise around the right needle tip.

TIP

To make a really neat cast-on edge, cast on one more stitch than instructed. Prepare to knit on a circular needle or set of double-pointed needles, (see pages 24–25), then slip the first cast-on stitch from the left needle onto the right. Lift the last cast-on stitch over the first and off the needle, in the same way as binding off (see page 30). Gently tighten the yarn. You now have the correct number of stitches, and the cast-on edge will have no little step where the first round begins.

3 Make a purl stitch
Draw the new loop away from you, back through the stitch. Allow the old loop to slip off the left needle tip. You now have one purl stitch on the right needle. Repeat Steps 1 through 3 until you reach the marker. One purl round is complete.

To purl a round: German (or Continental) method

This method of purling may be unfamiliar, but it can be very neat and speedy to work.

1 Bring yarn to front
Bring the yarn to the front of the work and hold it with your left hand, as shown.

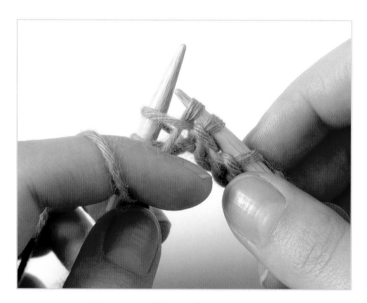

2 Insert needle, catch yarn
Insert the right needle as for the Scottish or English method, then insert it under the yarn in front of your left forefinger. Pull the yarn down with your left forefinger to tighten it gently. Use the right needle tip to draw the new loop back through the stitch, making a new purl stitch on the right needle.

3 Make a purl stitch
Allow the old stitch to slip off the left needle. One purl stitch is made on the right needle. Repeat Steps 2 and 3 until you reach the marker. One purl round is complete.

Double-pointed needles

The smooth round of this knitting is stockinette (all rounds knit), while the ridge is formed by a round of purl stitches. When you put aside work on double-pointed needles, push each set of stitches toward the centers of the needles, and lay the needles side by side. Use point protectors to prevent the stitches from slipping off the needles. The stitches should be arranged on three needles (from a set of four), or four needles (from a set of five), as on page 25. Use the empty fourth (or fifth) needle to begin the round.

To knit a round

3 Place a ring marker

Knit the stitches from the third needle in the same way. On the last needle of the round, knit to the last stitch, then slip a ring marker onto the right-hand needle and knit the last stitch. (You can't put the marker at the end of the last needle, or it will just fall off.) The last stitch of the round is always the stitch after a ring marker. Slip the marker from round to round as the work proceeds.

1 Knit with empty needle

Hold the needles and yarn in the way that suits you, with the empty needle behind the third needle (which holds the last stitch worked). Use the empty needle to knit each stitch from the first needle. As you approach the end of the first needle, it is helpful to alter the grip of your left hand to include the tip of the next needle, to prevent stretching the stitches between the two needles. Position the leading tip of the next needle above the tail end of the needle from which you are knitting.

2 Change to next needle

When all the stitches from the first needle have been knitted, that needle is empty. Take it in your right hand. Pull firmly on the yarn to make sure that the previous stitch is not loose, then use the empty needle to knit the stitches from the second needle, pulling the first stitch tightly to avoid making a gap between the needles.

To purl a round

Hold the work in the same way as for knitting a round, but bring the yarn to the front, then hold it and form the purl stitches in the same way as shown on a circular needle (see pages 27–28).

Binding off

When your knitting is complete, you need to bind off the stitches so that they are linked together and will not unravel. The process is the same for both circular and double-pointed needles.

Binding off knitwise

This is the most usual method of binding off, used to complete a piece of knitting in stockinette stitch.

1 Knit two stitches
Knit the first two stitches in the usual way. Insert the tip of the left needle from left to right, through the first stitch, as shown.

2 Lift first stitch over second
Lift the first stitch over the second and off the right-hand needle.

3 Repeat as required
Knit the next stitch. Repeat Steps 2 and 3 until one stitch remains at the end of the round (or bind off as many stitches as required).

4 Pull tail through last stitch
Cut the yarn about 6 in. (15 cm) from the needles, and pull it through the last stitch knitted. Thread the tail into a tapestry needle.

5 Finish the tail
Slip the needle under both threads of the next bound-off stitch to the left, then back through the previous stitch where the thread emerges, to make a looped stitch that resembles the other bound-off stitches. Run in the tail where it will not show (see page 33).

TIPS

- For a neat edge when binding off ribbing or another stitch pattern, work each stitch as knit or purl, to match the stitch beneath. This is often called "bind off in knit and purl as set."
- A bound-off edge usually stretches less than the rest of the knitting. In some instances—at the neck of a sweater, for example—a looser edge may be required. To achieve this, simply use a needle that is one or two sizes larger (any type of needle will do) in your right hand to knit or purl the stitches for the bind-off.

Binding off purlwise

Sometimes you need to bind off purlwise, to match previous rows, or when working a ribbed edge such as a neckband.

1 Purl two stitches
Purl two stitches in the usual way. Leave the yarn at the front of the work, toward you, and slip the tip of the left needle from left to right through the back of the first stitch.

2 Lift first stitch over second
Lift the first stitch over the second and off the right-hand needle. Purl the next stitch and repeat Steps 1 and 2 until one stitch remains at the end of the round. To finish, repeat Steps 4 and 5 of Binding Off Knitwise, opposite.

Using markers

There are several different types of markers you can use to help you keep your place when knitting in rounds.

Ring markers

Ring markers are small, slim plastic rings, available in various colors. Choose a size that fits the needles loosely, so the ring slips easily from one needle tip to the next. When you are working dart shapings (see pages 60–61) or complicated stitch patterns, you can use two or more colors—one to mark a shaping position or pattern repeat and another to mark the end of a round. To mark complete rounds on double-pointed needles, place the marker before the last stitch of the round; or use a threaded marker instead, as below.

Yarn loops

You can use short lengths of contrasting yarn, tied into small loops, as substitutes for ring markers. A smooth yarn such as double knitting cotton works well.

Split ring markers

Split rings are intended to mark a particular stitch in the knitting, as they can be removed and replaced at any time. For example, if your pattern instructs you to work a specific number of rounds, mark the first stitch of the first round with a split ring and leave it in place until you have worked the required number of rounds, so that you can count them up from the marker.

Threaded yarn marker

This method works well when knitting on double-pointed needles. Cut a length of a smooth, contrasting yarn about twice the height of the piece that you are knitting. Use a tapestry needle to thread it through the knitting between two stitches, where required. Tie a knot, leaving one short end and one long end. Work one round, then take the long tail through between the needles to the inside of the work. Work the next round, and bring the tail through between the needles, to the front. Repeat as required. To remove, undo the knot and gently pull out the thread.

Joining new yarn

If you run out of yarn and need to join in another ball, you can do this anywhere in circular knitting. There are no seams where you can hide the yarn tails, so try the technique below.

1 Tie on new yarn
Leaving tails at least 6 in. (15 cm) long on both the old yarn and the new, tie the yarn from the new ball around the old with a single knot and slide the knot up close to the work.

2 Unpick the knot
Continue knitting with the new yarn. When the work is complete unpick the knot and run in the tails as shown on the striped example, opposite.

Knitting stripes

If you want to knit stripes, it is usual to begin and end them at the beginning of a round. If the stripes are narrow (one to four rounds), you can carry a color up the inside of the work. For wider stripes, it is best to cut the yarn and join it, as shown above. The technique is the same whether you are working on a circular needle or on a set of double-pointed needles.

1 Join in the new color
Join the second color to the first with a simple knot at the beginning of a round, as shown above. (Only cut the first color if you are not going to carry it up and use it again.)

2 Unpick the knots

When the knitting is complete, unpick the knots on the inside.

3 Run in the new color

Thread the right-hand tail (the new color) into a tapestry needle and run it in to the left, up and down along the first round of stitches of the same color, matching the path of the yarn through the stitches. Do this for about 2 in. (5 cm). Stretch the knitting between your fingers to make sure that the tail is no tighter than the stitches, then trim off any excess yarn.

4 Run in the old color

Thread the left-hand tail (the old color) into a tapestry needle and run it in to the right in the same way, along the last round of stitches of the same color.

Step hardly shows

Here, the tails of the lower color change (from yellow to blue) have been run in as above, while the tails of the upper color change (from blue back to yellow) have not yet been dealt with. Note how running in the tails correctly helps reduce the step where the colors change.

TIPS

For bulky yarns

When you are knitting in bulky yarn, you need to reduce the bulk of each run-in tail. Untwist the tail and snip away half the strands, quite close to the work.

Run in the remaining strands to left and right, as shown above.

Increasing

There are several ways to increase (make extra stitches), and the method chosen will affect the appearance of your knitting. Here are four common increases.

Knit twice in the same stitch (Ktw)

This method forms a little "bar" on the surface of the knitting, enabling you easily to count the rows between increases when shaping, for example, a sleeve.

1 Knit into front loop
Knit into the front loop of the next stitch in the usual way, but leave it on the left-hand needle.

2 Knit into back loop
Now knit into the back loop of the same stitch, dropping it from the left-hand needle.

One extra stitch made
This method makes a firm extra stitch. Here, three increases have been made on alternate rounds. Each increase shows as a little horizontal bar beneath the extra stitch.

Make one (m1)

This increase method leaves a small hole in the knitting, which may be used to accentuate a shaping, or as part of a lace pattern.

2 Knit into new loop
Knit into the new loop in the usual way.

One extra stitch made
Here, three extra stitches have been made on alternate rounds. A small hole is formed at the base of each new stitch.

1 Lift horizontal thread
Use the left needle tip to lift the horizontal thread lying before the next stitch, making a new loop on the left needle.

Make one through back loop
(m1tbl)

Sometimes called the "invisible increase," this method leaves no hole in the knitting.

One extra stitch made
Here, three stitches have been increased by this method, on alternate rounds. The extra stitches are less noticeable because there are no visible bars or holes.

Lift thread and knit into back loop
As for Make One (above), lift the thread before the next stitch onto the left-hand needle, but then insert the right-hand needle through the loop from right to back left, and knit it. This is called "knit through the back loop."

Yarn over (yo)

This increase is often used in lace stitch patterns, because it makes a visible hole in the fabric. It can also be used to make a row of eyelet holes for a drawstring or ribbon. In both cases, the increased stitch is usually balanced by a corresponding decrease (see pages 38–39), unless extra stitches are required to shape the knitting. The method of making the yarn over varies depending on whether the stitches at either side are knitted or purled.

Yarn over between two knit stitches

Bring the yarn toward you between the needle tips and take it over the top of the right-hand needle, making an extra loop on the right-hand needle. The yarn is at the back of the work, ready to knit the next stitch.

Yarn over between a knit and a purl stitch

After a knit stitch, the yarn is at the back of the work. Bring it to the front, between the needles, then carry it over the top of the right-hand needle and through to the front again, making an extra loop. The yarn is wrapped counterclockwise around the right needle, and is now in position to purl the next stitch.

Yarn over between two purl stitches

After working a purl stitch, the yarn is at the front of the work. Carry it away from you over the top of the right-hand needle and back to the front again between the two needles, making an extra loop on the right-hand needle. The yarn is at the front of the work, ready to purl the next stitch.

Yarn over between a purl and a knit stitch

After purling a stitch, the yarn is at the front. Take it across the top of the right-hand needle to the back, creating an extra loop on the right-hand needle. The yarn is now at the back, ready to knit the next stitch.

See pages 116–117 for examples of stitch patterns using yarn overs combined with various types of decrease (see pages 38–39) to make lace stitch patterns.

Slipping stitches knitwise and purlwise

Slip stitches are used when working decreases, as shown on pages 38–39, and for certain stitch patterns. These stitches may need to be slipped either knitwise or purlwise, depending on the pattern instructions.

Also, in circular knitting you sometimes need to slip stitches onto a stitch holder, or from one needle to another, to rejoin the yarn at a different place. These stitches should always be slipped purlwise to prevent twisting.

Slip one knitwise
(S1, Sl1 or Sl1k)

1 Insert needle as if to knit
Insert the right needle into the next stitch from left to right, in the same way as when knitting a stitch.

2 Slip stitch from left to right needle
Slip the stitch from the left needle onto the right. The stitch is twisted. This slipped stitch is used for some methods of decreasing (see pages 38–39) and also in some stitch patterns.

Slip one purlwise
(S1p or Sl1p)

1 Insert needle as if to purl
Insert the right needle into the next stitch from right to left, in the same way as when purling a stitch.

2 Slip stitch from left to right needle
Slip the stitch from the left needle onto the right. The stitch is not twisted. Always use this method when arranging stitches on double-pointed needles or when slipping stitches onto holders (see page 53). The technique is also used in some stitch patterns.

Decreasing

There are numerous ways of working two (or more) stitches together to decrease the total number. Each method has a different appearance, making a stitch that slopes to the right or to the left. In circular knitting, the right side of the work is always facing you, so the three decreases shown below are the most useful.

Knit two together (K2tog)

This is the commonest method of decreasing. It makes a decrease that slants to the right.

1 Insert needle through two stitches together

Insert the right needle tip into the first two stitches on the left needle, from left to right.

2 Knit two together
Wrap the yarn as for a knit stitch and knit the two stitches together, slipping them both off the left-hand needle. One stitch has been decreased.

This decrease slopes to the right
After completing the round and knitting another, the decrease can be seen to slope to the right. Here, a series of decreases has been arranged to form a sloping line.

TIP

When working on a set of double-pointed needles, always arrange the stitches so that the two or three stitches required to work each decrease are all on the same needle. If you need to re-arrange the stitches, always slip them purlwise (see page 37).

Slip, slip, knit (Ssk)

This method makes a neat decrease that slants to the left.

1 Slip two stitches knitwise

Insert the right needle tip into the next stitch from left to right, as if to knit, and slip it onto the right needle. Slip the next stitch in the same way.

2 Wrap yarn and lift stitches over

Insert the left needle tip through both the slipped stitches, from left to right. Carry the yarn counterclockwise around the right needle tip and lift the two stitches together over the yarn, leaving one stitch on the right needle. One stitch has been decreased.

This decrease slopes to the left

This decrease shows as a stitch sloping to the left. Again, a series of decreases can be arranged to form a sloping line.

Double decrease (S2togk)

This method of decreasing two stitches at the same time slants neither to the right nor to the left.

1 Slip two stitches together knitwise

Insert the right needle tip from left to right into the next two stitches, as if to knit two together (see opposite) and slip both stitches onto the right needle.

2 Knit one, lift slipped stitches over

Knit the next stitch in the usual way. Then use the left needle to lift both slipped stitches together, over the knit stitch and off the right needle. Two stitches have been decreased.

This decrease does not slope

This double decrease slopes neither to left nor right. A series of such decreases can be arranged to form a vertical line, ideal for dart shapings in circular knitting.

Assembly

The techniques used in circular knitting are designed to avoid sewing seams. Seamless garments are flexible and comfortable, with no weak points liable to come apart. To knit without seams, learn the techniques of Grafting and Binding Off Together (below). See also Picking Up Stitches on pages 54–55.

Grafting (Kitchener stitch)

Grafting is a method of replicating a row of knitted stitches using a needle and yarn, making an "invisible" join with no extra bulk. It is shown here on the toe of a sock, where two sets of stitches are placed side by side and grafted together, but the same method may be used to join any two separate edges, providing each has the same number of stitches. The grafting here is shown in blue for clarity. Working with the stitches threaded onto two lengths of contrasting yarn (green), as shown, makes it easier to match the stitch size for an invisible join. However, you can also work grafting with the stitches arranged on two needles.

Always use a tapestry needle (see page 12) with a blunt tip to avoid splitting the stitches.

1 Slip stitches onto lengths of yarn
The edge(s) to be joined should not be bound off. Thread a tapestry needle with a length of smooth, contrasting yarn (such as double knitting cotton) and slip the stitches from one edge purlwise onto the yarn from the needle or stitch holder (see page 53). Thread the stitches from the opposite edge onto another length of yarn.

3 Take thread down and up through upper stitches
Take the needle down through the center of the stitch at upper right, and bring it up through the next upper stitch to the left. Pull through, not too tightly.

2 Bring thread up at stitch center
Cut a length of knitting yarn about three times as long as the edge to be grafted, or use a long tail left at the end of the knitting. We have used a length of yarn in a contrasting color, so that you can see the method clearly, but if possible, use the long tail from the knitting. Thread it into the tapestry needle, bring the needle up through the center of the first stitch at lower right, and pull through. If you are using a separate length of yarn, as here, leave a 6-in. (15-cm) tail on the surface, to be run in later on the wrong side of the work.

4 Take thread down and up through lower stitches

Take the needle down again through the center of the same lower stitch (where it emerged), and up through the next lower stitch to the left. Pull through.

5 Repeat to the left

Repeat Steps 3 and 4 to the left, pulling each stitch gently so that the size matches the knitted stitches.

6 Run in tail(s), pull out threads

At the end, run in the tail on the wrong side of the work (see page 33). If there is a starting tail, run that in too. Gently pull out the contrasting cotton threads. The grafted stitches should be indistinguishable from a row of knitted stitches.

Bind-off together

Two sets of stitches on two separate needles may also be bound off together making a firm seam. This method may be used to close the base of a purse or the underarm of a sweater, as shown here. When the stitches are knitted up for the yoke, groups of stitches are left on holders at each underarm and long yarn tails are left, which are used to work this bind-off on the inside of the sweater. There should be the same number of stitches on each side of the opening.

1 Arrange stitches on two needles

Slip the stitches purlwise onto two double-pointed needles (see page 37). There should be the same number of stitches on each needle. Hold the two needles side by side in your left hand, with the working yarn at the right.

2 Knit two together

Insert an empty needle knitwise through the first stitch on the front needle and the first stitch on the back needle, wrap the yarn in the usual way, and knit both stitches together.

3 Knit next two together

Knit the next two stitches together in the same way.

4 Bind off

Lift the first new stitch over the second, in the same way as for binding off (see page 30), using one of the needles in your left hand.

5 Repeat as required

Repeat Steps 3 and 4 to the end. Cut the yarn, leaving a 6-in. (15-cm) tail, and pull it through the last stitch. Run in the tail securely on the wrong side in the usual way (see page 33).

Gauge

Most knitting patterns quote a recommended gauge—that is, the number of stitches and rows (or rounds) to a certain measurement. Your pattern may tell you, for example, that the gauge is 18 stitches and 24 rounds to 4 inches (10 cm), measured over stockinette. If the gauge of your knitting does not match that on the pattern, your knitting will be too big or too small.

To check gauge

To be entirely sure that you have chosen the right needle size in circular knitting, you need to knit quite a large sample—especially if you are using a circular needle. Knitting a sample in rows on single-pointed needles will not necessarily give a true indication of the gauge in circular knitting. Use the same yarn that you will use for the project, and a circular needle or set of double-pointed needles the same size as required for the project. (You can, however, use a shorter length of needle than that specified for the project, provided it is the same brand.)

2 Count the stitches

Lay the sample flat and insert two pins, 4 in. (10 cm) apart, across a straight row of stitches at the center of the piece. Count the number of stitches between the pins.

1 Knit a sample tube

Cast on enough stitches to comfortably fill the circular needle, or on double-pointed needles enough for a tube about 10 in. (25 cm) all around. Work in rounds of the required stitch (often stockinette, as shown here) for about 6 in. (15 cm). You do not need to bind off; thread the stitches onto a length of smooth cotton yarn with a tapestry needle, and tie the ends. You can then leave the ball of yarn attached to the gauge sample and, if you need the yarn later, unpick the gauge sample to complete the project. Block the sample piece in the same way as you intend to block the finished project (see page 45).

3 Count the rounds

Then insert the pins across a vertical line of stitches, 4 in. (10 cm) apart, and count the number of rounds between the pins.

If you have too many stitches or rounds to 4 in. (10 cm), your knitting is too tight, and you should try another sample using a larger needle. If you have too few stitches or rounds, your knitting is too loose, and you should try again using a smaller needle.

Keeping count

Keeping count of stitches and rounds in circular knitting can be confusing. Study the section on Using Markers (see page 31). You can also use a row-counting device (see page 13), or keep a note of each completed round with paper and pencil.

Measuring work in progress

In circular knitting, it is practically impossible to measure the width of work in progress with any accuracy. That's why correct gauge (see opposite) is so important.

If you need to measure the length, lay the work as flat as you can without stretching it and use a tape measure.

Gauge is affected by:

- The thickness and type of yarn, and its fiber. Two yarns of equal thickness may knit at different gauges because one is more slippery, more tightly spun, or more elastic than the other.
- The size and type of needles you choose. The larger the needle size, the larger the stitch—but the use of plastic, metal, or wooden needles may also affect gauge, because of their relative smoothness. Gauge may differ between a circular needle and a set of double-pointed needles of the same size, because of the slightly different grip adopted by the knitter.
- The way you knit. Some people hold the yarn more tightly than others.
- The stitch pattern. If the instructions are for a project in a particular stitch, the gauge is usually quoted for this stitch and should be checked in the same way.

Therefore, it is most important to check your gauge for every new project, and to match it to the knitting instructions as closely as possible.

TIPS

- If you buy extra yarn for your project, you can knit a small item such as this drawstring purse (see pages 50–51) and use it as a gauge sample. Use the needle(s) you intend to use for the main project; the finished size of the purse will vary depending on the yarn and needle(s).

- Start a project by knitting a sleeve or other smaller part. Re-check the gauge as opposite. If it is correct, you can slip the stitches from the smooth yarn back onto the needle(s) and continue knitting. If not correct, you must unravel the work and start again with a different needle size.

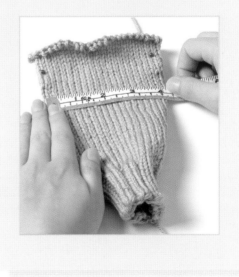

Following knitting instructions

Knitting instructions for circular knitting are similar to instructions for knitting in rows, and should be carefully followed in the same way. Read through the instructions before you begin to make sure that you understand the method of construction and any abbreviations used.

Sizes and measurements

Choose the size you need from the table at the beginning of the pattern.

Decide whether to work in inches or centimeters throughout. Never switch from one set of measurements to another during the course of a project, as they do not coincide exactly.

In this book, the instructions for different sizes are given in square brackets: **1st size** [2nd size, **3rd size**, 4th size] etc.

Materials

The yarn required for each project is described not only by type (e.g. Aran-weight yarn), but also by yardage, to enable you to use any similar yarn with a similar yardage (see page 9).

The needle sizes given are the recommended size. After checking your gauge (see page 42), you may need to select a different size.

Gauge

Always check your own gauge (see page 42).

Repeats

Asterisks indicate a series of stitches to be repeated. For example, "* K2, P1 * repeat from * to * 3 more times" means you should work the three stitches given, then repeat them three times more.

Instructions in round brackets should be repeated the number of times specified after the brackets. For example, "(K2, P1) twice" means K2, P1, K2, P1.

Double asterisks (**) and triple asterisks (***) are used to indicate whole sections of a pattern that are repeated elsewhere. For example, if you come across the symbol **—perhaps in the body of a sweater—it means that further on in the instructions you will be told to "Knit as body from ** to end" (or, from ** to ***).

Abbreviations

Abbreviations may vary slightly from one pattern source to another; these are the abbreviations used in this book.

alt	alternate	PB	purl bobble (page 73)
beg	beginning	psso	pass slip stitch over
C	cable (page 72)	P2tog	purl 2 together
col	color	rev St st	reverse stockinette stitch (reverse stocking stitch) (page 106)
cm(s)	centimeter(s)	rib	ribbing
dec(s)	decrease(s), decreasing (pages 38–39)	rd(s)	round(s)
DK	double knitting	RS	right side (of work)
dpn	double-pointed needle(s)	Sl1k	slip 1 knitwise (page 37)
foll	following	Sl1p	slip 1 purlwise (page 37)
g	gram(s)	sl st	slip stitch
in(s)	inch(es)	st(s)	stitch(es)
inc(s)	increase(s), increasing (pages 34–36)	Ssk	slip, slip, knit (page 39)
K	knit (page 26)	S2togk	slip two together, knit one, pass slipped sts over (page 39)
Ktw	knit into front and back of same stitch (page 34)	St st	stockinette stitch (stocking stitch) (page 106)
K2tog	knit 2 together (page 38)	tbl	through back loop(s)
m	meter	tog	together
MSB	make small bobble (page 73)	Tw2L	left twist (page 70)
mm	millimeter	Tw2R	right twist (page 71)
m1	make one (page 35)	WS	wrong side (of work)
m1tbl	make one through back loop (page 35)	yd	yard
P	purl (pages 27–28)	yo	yarn over needle to make extra stitch (page 36)

Blocking

This final process will help you achieve a professional finish to your knitting, by settling the stitches evenly.

Circular knits can be difficult to press by the usual method used for flat knitting, and there are rarely any seams that require pressing. Gently washing circular knits and drying them flat will help to even out any tight or loose stitches. Be sure to use a gentle detergent suitable for the yarn you have used. You will also need two large towels.

1 Squeeze gently
Add a small amount of specialist detergent to a bowl of lukewarm water and dissolve thoroughly. Put the knit in the water and squeeze the suds gently through it. Leave to soak for two or three minutes.

2 Drain away the water
Do not lift or wring out the knit, but support it with your hand as you drain away the water.

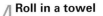

4 Roll in a towel
Squeeze out the excess water (do not wring) and lay the knit flat on a large towel. Roll up the towel and squeeze it hard to blot away more moisture.

3 Rinse
Rinse thoroughly, handling gently as before, in three changes of cool water.

5 Dry flat
Arrange the knit flat on a second towel, patting it into shape. Leave it to dry completely, away from direct sunlight.

chapter two
Projects & Special Techniques

The projects in this section are arranged in order of the skill level required, beginning with a simple cowl scarf and ending with circular-knitted sweaters for all the family. Helpful tips include suggestions for adapting the project instructions by, for example, working in stripes or adding two-color patterns or textured stitches, so that you can create your own unique designs.

Along the way, special techniques are required to complete some of the projects, and these are shown step by step.

Gauge and finished size are not crucial for articles such as the scarf, purse, bag, toys, and pillows, so you can simply choose a yarn of the recommended weight and start knitting. However, garments such as the hat, mittens, gloves, and sweaters require careful measuring and accurate gauge (see page 42).

Project 1: Loopy scarf

If you've never knitted on a circular needle before, try this simple but unusual design. The scarf is a continuous loop of knitting. Wear it wound twice around the neck for a flattering "cowl" effect, to keep you snug in the coldest weather.

Finished size: Approx. 48 in. (120 cm) around x 7 in. (17.5 cm) deep

MATERIALS

- Approx. 8 oz (200 gm) bulky-weight yarn (approx. 125 yds/114 metres to 100 gm)
- Circular needle, size US 11 (8 mm), length 24 in. (60 cm) or 32 in. (80 cm)
- One ring marker
- Tapestry needle to suit yarn

Gauge
12 stitches and 16 rounds to 4 in. (10 cm) measured over stockinette stitch, using size US 11 (8 mm) needles. Gauge is not crucial provided a change in size is acceptable, but if the gauge is too loose, you may need more yarn.

Making the scarf

Using a size US 11 (8 mm) circular needle, cast on 144 sts. Arrange in a circle without twisting (see page 24). Slip ring marker onto right-hand needle tip. All rounds begin and end at this marker. Slip it at the beginning of every round.
Purl 5 rounds.
Knit 5 rounds.
Repeat these 10 rounds three more times.
40 rounds in all.
Bind off.

ASSEMBLY

Use tapestry needle to run in tails (see page 33). Block (see page 45).

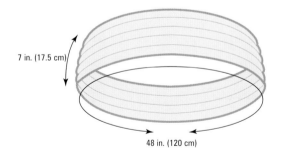

7 in. (17.5 cm)

48 in. (120 cm)

See also:

Preparing to Knit (page 24)
Using Markers (page 31)
Running In Tails (page 33)
Blocking (page 45)
Abbreviations (page 44)

For your first circular knitting project, try this very simple loopy scarf. The ridges formed by a sequence of knit and purl rounds naturally fall into cozy folds around your neck.

TIPS

- Select a textured or shade-dyed yarn for your scarf: you only need a small amount, so choose something exciting!
- Try knitting this scarf in stripes of two or more colors (see pages 32–33).

Project 2: Drawstring purse

For your first project using a set of double-pointed needles, try making this simple purse. It's just a tube of knitting, with a row of holes to take a drawstring, joined at the lower edge.

Finished size: Approx. 4½ x 6 in. (11.5 x 15 cm)

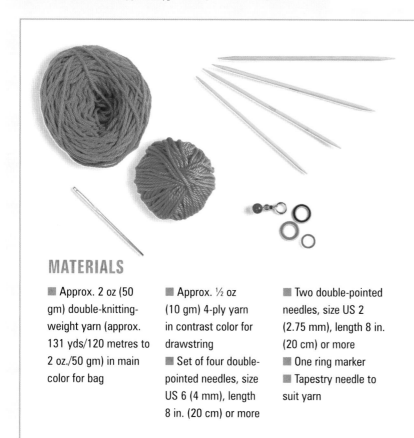

MATERIALS

■ Approx. 2 oz (50 gm) double-knitting-weight yarn (approx. 131 yds/120 metres to 2 oz./50 gm) in main color for bag

■ Approx. ½ oz (10 gm) 4-ply yarn in contrast color for drawstring
■ Set of four double-pointed needles, size US 6 (4 mm), length 8 in. (20 cm) or more

■ Two double-pointed needles, size US 2 (2.75 mm), length 8 in. (20 cm) or more
■ One ring marker
■ Tapestry needle to suit yarn

Gauge
22 stitches and 28 rounds to 4 in. (10 cm) measured over stockinette stitch, using size US 6 (4 mm) needles. Gauge is not crucial provided a change in size is acceptable, but too loose a gauge will make a purse that stretches in use, and extra yarn may be required.

Making the purse
BEGIN AT TOP EDGE:
Using two of four size US 6 (4 mm) double-pointed needles and main yarn, cast on 49 sts. Arrange sts on three needles: 16 sts/16 sts/17 sts (ending with first cast-on stitch). Arrange in a triangle without twisting (see pages 24–25), with 17 sts on left-hand needle. Slip first cast-on st from left-hand needle to right-hand needle, lift last cast-on st over it and off needle. 48 sts, arranged 16 sts/16 sts/16 sts.

Round 1: P to last st, place ring marker on right-hand needle, P last st. All rounds begin and end 1 st after this marker. Slip it on every round.
Purl 3 rounds.
Knit 4 rounds.
Purl 4 rounds.
Knit 1 round.

9 in. (23 cm)

6 in. (15 cm)

See also:
Yarn Over (yo), page 36
Bind-off Together, page 41
Abbreviations, page 44

MAKE ROW OF HOLES

Round 14: K1, * K2tog, yo, ssk, K2, *, repeat from * to * six more times, K2tog, yo, ssk, K1, ending 1 st after round marker. 8 holes made.

Round 15: K2, * K into front and back of yo, K4, *, repeat from * to * six more times, K into front and back of yo, K2. 48 sts.

Knit 1 round.

Purl 4 rounds.

Continue in stockinette stitch (all rounds knit) until bag measures 6 in. (15 cm) in all, or the required length, ending 1 st after round marker.

CLOSE LOWER EDGE

Slip last 24 sts of previous round onto one needle. Slip remaining 24 sts onto another needle. Place the two needles side by side and bind off together (see page 41).

MAKING THE DRAWSTRING

Using two US size 2 (2.75 mm) double-pointed needles and contrast yarn, cast on 5 sts and work an I-cord (see page 98) about 16 in. (40 cm) long. Bind off.

ASSEMBLY

Run in any remaining tails on purse (see page 33). Block (see page 45). Thread one tail of drawstring into tapestry needle and run it in and out of the row of holes, beginning and ending at the center of one side. Run in drawstring tails down the center of the drawstring. Gather up drawstring and tie in a bow.

The purse is formed from a tube, knitted from the top edge downward, and the drawstring is an I-cord.

TIPS

- You can make this bag in any weight of yarn that you choose. Use the recommended needle size for the main part of the bag. In aran-weight yarn, the bag will measure about 6 in. (15 cm) across, so knit to a total length of about 7½ in. (19 cm), and make the drawstring about 20 in. (50 cm) long. In a chunky yarn, the width will be about 8 in. (20 cm), so make the length about 10 in. (25 cm), with a 24-in. (60-cm) drawstring.
- Use this pattern to test your gauge for a larger project (see page 43).
- Try adding a fringe to the lower edge (see page 99), or decorate the ends of the drawstring with pompons (see pages 102–103) or tassels (see pages 100–101).
- Try knitting the main part of the bag in a textured stitch (diagonal rib on page 111 shown on the right-hand bag), or with one or more bands of fairisle pattern. Any pattern requiring a multiple of 3, 4, 6, or 8 sts will suit these instructions.

Provisional cast-on

This technique is sometimes called the "waste yarn cast-on." It is used to begin a project in the middle, such as the shoulder bag on pages 56–57. After completing the top part of the project, stitches are picked up from above the provisional cast-on. These stitches may then be bound off together to close a seam (see page 41), or worked downward to make a border or to shape the lower part of the project. After completion, the waste yarn is removed.

Waste yarn

For the waste yarn, choose a smooth yarn such as sport weight or double knitting cotton, preferably a little finer than the project yarn. Use the same needle(s) that you will use for the main part of the project.

1 Cast on with waste yarn
Using either the Long-tail or Cable cast-on (see pages 20–23), cast on the required number of stitches, join them into a circle, and knit one round in the usual way. This single round makes the provisional cast-on easy to remove. Cut the waste yarn, leaving a 6-in. (15-cm) tail, and join in the main yarn. Complete the top part of the article.

3 Remove waste yarn
Complete the lower part of the project as required. Unpick the knot joining the main yarn to the waste yarn. Carefully snip through the stitches of the single round knitted in waste yarn, about every ten stitches or so, and gently pull out all the waste yarn. Run in the tails of main yarn on the wrong side (see page 33). In stockinette stitch, the join is invisible.

2 Pick up stitches
Turn the work upside down and roll the cast-on edge to the outside, so that you can see the loops of the first round of stitches in the main yarn. Using a needle (or set of needles) of the correct size and the main yarn, knit up one stitch from each loop of the first main yarn round, in a similar way to Picking Up Stitches (see pages 56–57).

See Also
- Cuddly Shoulder Bag **p56**
- Pillows **p74**
- Snake **p90**

Using stitch holders

Stitch holders are similar to large safety pins. They are made of plastic or metal, but have a blunt point that will not split the yarn. Use a stitch holder to temporarily hold a group of stitches while you knit further rounds (or rows) on the remaining stitches—for example when working an opening for a mitten thumb (see pages 58–59), or the heel of a sock (see pages 55–57).

To make an opening

When working gloves (see pages 78–81), mittens (see pages 58–59), or our glove puppets (pages 84–87), you need to work an opening in the knitting at the base of the thumb. At a later stage, stitches are picked up (see pages 54–55) around the opening to work the thumb. Omitting Step 2 will make an opening in the form of a slit.

1 Slip stitches to holder
At the base of the opening, knit across the stitches to be held, and then slip them onto a holder. Fasten the holder. The working yarn is at the left of the holder, ready to knit the rows required to form the sides of the opening.

3 Bridge the gap
At the top of the opening, bridge the gap with the required number of stitches, cast on by the Simple Thumb method (see page 23). Continue working in rounds, as instructed.

2 Selvage stitches
The sides of the opening are formed by working backward and forward in rows, not rounds. These rows are often knitted with a selvage stitch at each end, to make a neat edge that is easy to work into at a later stage. A simple selvage is worked by knitting the first and last stitch of every row, as shown here.

Alternative holders
- Two or three stitches may be held with a hairgrip or split ring. Safety pins may also be used, but take care not to split the yarn with the sharp point.
- Larger groups of stitches may be left on a spare double-pointed needle. Choose one that is a size smaller than the needles you are using, but not too short, so the stitches don't slip off easily. Alternatively, push point protectors (or corks) onto the needle tips.
- Large groups of stitches may also be slipped onto a length of smooth yarn threaded into a tapestry needle. Knot the two ends of the yarn to prevent the stitches from slipping off.

Picking up stitches

When constructing gloves and mittens, (and also socks and neckbands), you often need to pick up stitches: from a holder, a side edge, or a cast-on edge. The example below shows stitches picked up around a small hole, onto double-pointed needles.

Knitting stitches from a holder

Knitting directly from a holder can be awkward, so slip the stitches onto an extra double-pointed needle.

1 Slip stitches to a spare needle

Use a needle that is one or two sizes smaller than the size you are knitting with, to prevent stretching the stitches. Insert the needle point from left to right, as shown, through each stitch in turn to prevent twisting the stitches.

2 Knit from spare needle

Then knit the stitches from the spare needle.

Picking up stitches from a side edge

Where the side edges of a hole have been formed by knitting in rows you will need to pick up a number of stitches from the row ends.

1 Insert in side edge

Insert the needle tip one whole stitch in from the edge of the knitting, so that there are two strands of yarn across the top of the needle.

2 Form the new stitch

Wrap the yarn in the usual way and draw the new stitch through, allowing the side edge to slip off the needle. Repeat as required.

TIPS

- Sometimes there are more stitches on a bound-off or cast-on edge than you are instructed to pick up. For a neat finish, pick up one new stitch from each edge stitch, then decrease (see pages 38–39) to the required number on the next round.
- For a neat, flat join, the number of stitches picked up from a side edge is normally about three quarters the number of rows. If your join looks gappy, try again, picking up one stitch from each row end, and then decrease to the required number of stitches on the next round.

Picking up stitches from a cast-on edge

The top edge of a hole is usually formed by casting on a group of stitches, so you need to pick up stitches from the lower loops of the cast-on stitches.

1 Insert between stitches, wrap yarn
Working along a cast-on edge made by the Simple Thumb method (see page 23), insert the needle through a single loop of the cast-on edge. Wrap the yarn around the needle in the usual way. (If the edge is cast on by a firmer method, insert the needle between two stitches. The cast-on edge will form a ridge on the wrong side of the work.)

2 Draw the stitch through
Draw the new loop through, allowing the cast-on edge to slip off the needle. You have made a new stitch on the right needle.

3 Repeat
Repeat as required, making one new stitch in every cast-on stitch.

Complete the circle

You now need to pick up another group of new stitches down the remaining side edge of the hole.

Pick up from remaining edge
To make this thumb, you need to pick up another set of stitches from the remaining side edge. The stitches may then be arranged evenly (or as instructed) on the needles, and the thumb completed as required.

Picking up stitches from a bound-off edge

Sometimes, pattern instructions will tell you to pick up stitches from a bound-off edge.

Insert needle, wrap yarn
With the right side of the work facing you, work along the edge from right to left. Insert the needle through the loop of the first stitch, just below the bind-off, and wrap the yarn around the needle in the usual way. Draw the new loop through, making a new stitch on the needle. Repeat as required.

See Also
- Mittens **p58**
- Gloves **p78**
- Kitten toy **p84**

Project 3: Cuddly shoulder bag

Practice your circular knitting by making this unusual bag. As it can be knitted in just a few evenings, you'll soon feel at home knitting "in the round." The bowl-shaped base is knitted downward, decreasing with darts (see pages 60–61).

Finished size: Width 11 in. (28 cm), height 22 in. (56 cm)

MATERIALS

- ▪ Approx. 11 oz (300 gm) bulky yarn (approx. 125 yds/114 metres to 100 gm)
- ▪ Small ball of waste yarn

- ▪ Circular needle, size US 8 (5 mm), length 16 in. (40 cm)
- ▪ Set of four double-pointed needles, size US 8 (5 mm), length 8 in. (20 cm)

- ▪ One ring marker
- ▪ Tapestry needle to suit yarn

Gauge
18 stitches and 24 rounds to 4 in. (10 cm) measured over stockinette stitch, using size US 8 (5 mm) needles. Check your gauge as shown on page 42.
Gauge is not crucial provided a change in size is acceptable, but if your gauge is too loose extra yarn may be required. Note that this gauge is firmer than the

recommended gauge for this type of yarn, in order to make a sturdy bag with minimum stretch.
Note: If you prefer, you can substitute double-pointed needles, 12 in. (30 cm) in length, for the circular needle, dividing the stitches evenly between three needles and placing the ring marker before the last stitch of the round.

Making the bag

The main part of the bag is begun with a provisional cast-on using waste yarn, and knitted upward to the top. The shaped base is knitted last, working downward from the waste yarn (see page 52).
Using the circular needle and waste yarn cast on 96 sts.
Arrange the stitches in a circle without twisting (see page 24) and Knit 1 round, placing a ring marker on the right-hand needle after knitting the last stitch.
Change to main yarn and Knit 36 rounds, ending at marker.

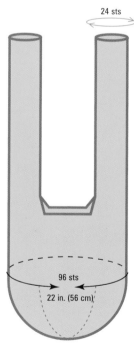

SHAPE FIRST HANDLE
The base of the handle is knitted backward and forward in rows:
* **Row 1:** Using a double-pointed needle, ssk, K32, K2tog, turn. Work on these 34 sts only, leaving remaining sts on circular needle.
Row 2: Using a second double-pointed needle, P34.

Row 3: Ssk, K to last 2 sts, K2tog.
Row 4: P to end.
Repeat rows 3 and 4 four more times. 24 sts.
The remainder of the handle is knitted in rounds:
Round 1: K 8 sts onto each of three double-pointed needles, slipping ring marker onto right-hand needle before knitting last stitch.
Continue in rounds until tubular part of handle measures 16 in. (41.5 cm), ending 1 st after marker. Bind off, removing marker *.

SHAPE SECOND HANDLE

Return to sts left on circular needle. Thread tapestry needle with waste yarn and slip through next 12 sts to left of base of first handle. Knot ends of waste yarn.
Rejoin main yarn at right of remaining sts and work as First Handle from * to *. (You may wish to slip the remaining 12 sts from the circular needle onto another length of waste yarn.)

BORDER TO OPENING

With right side of work facing, using the set of four double-pointed needles, ** K 12 sts from length of waste yarn at center front (see page 54), pick up and K 10 sts from first side edge of handle (see page 54), pick up and K 10 sts from second side edge of handle, ** repeat from ** to ** once more, placing a ring marker before last st. 64 sts.
Knit 5 rounds, ending 1 st after marker.
Bind off loosely, removing marker.

SHAPE BASE

Turn the work upside down. With right side of work facing, using size US 8 (5 mm) double-pointed needles and main yarn, pick up and K 96 sts from loops of first row in main yarn (see page 52), putting 32 sts on each of three needles.
Round 1: * K6, K2tog, ssk, K6, *, repeat * to * five more times, placing a ring marker on right-hand needle before last stitch. Slip this marker on every round. 84 sts.
Knit 5 rounds.
Round 7: * K5, K2tog, ssk, K5, *, repeat * to * five more times. 72 sts.
Knit 5 rounds.
Round 13: * K4, K2tog, ssk, K4, *, repeat * to * five more times. 60 sts.
Knit 3 rounds.
Round 17: * K3, K2tog, ssk, K3, * repeat * to * five more times. 48 sts.
Knit 3 rounds.
Round 21: * K2, K2tog, ssk, K2, * repeat * to * five more times. 36 sts.
Knit 3 rounds.

Round 25: * K1, K2tog, ssk, K1, * repeat * to * five more times. 24 sts.
Knit 1 round.
Round 27: * K2tog, ssk, * repeat * to * five more times. 12 sts.
Bind off. Cut yarn, leaving an 8-in. (20-cm) tail.

ASSEMBLY

Remove the waste yarn cast-on. (It is easier to unpick the single round than the cast-on edge itself—see page 52.)
Thread tail at center of base into tapestry needle and run it through the last round of sts, gathering them up tightly to close the central hole, in same way as for the Hat on page 61. Secure the yarn tail on the inside with several backstitches around the hole. Run in all other yarn tails (see page 33).
Tie the two handles with a firm reef knot, leaving free ends about 2½ in. (6 cm) long.
Block (see page 45).

See also:
Provisional Cast-on (page 52)
Picking up Stitches (pages 54–55)
Abbreviations (page 44)

The perfect slouchy shoulder bag, it is roomy enough to fit all your essentials, and you can easily adjust the length of the handle to suit. The main part of the bag is begun on waste yarn, and knitted upward to the top. The shaped base is knitted last, working downward from the waste yarn.

TYING THE HANDLES

Tie the two handles with a firm reef knot, leaving free ends of about 2½ in. (6 cm).

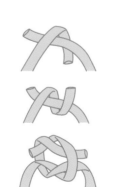

1

2

3

4

Project 4: Mittens

These cozy mittens come in three sizes, to fit all members of the family. They're quick to knit in aran-weight yarn, using double-pointed needles, with no fiddly seams to sew.

Finished size: To fit hand measured from wrist to middle finger tip: 6 in. (15 cm); 7 in. (17.5 cm); 8 in. (20 cm)

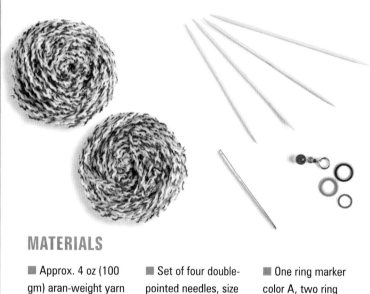

MATERIALS

- Approx. 4 oz (100 gm) aran-weight yarn (approx. 94 yds/85 metres to 2 oz/50 gm)

- Set of four double-pointed needles, size US 7 (4.5 mm), length 8 in. (20 cm)

- One ring marker color A, two ring markers color B
- One stitch holder
- Tapestry needle to suit yarn

Gauge
18 stitches and 24 rounds to 4 in. (10 cm) measured over stockinette stitch, using size US 7 (4.5 mm) needles. Check gauge as shown on page 42. Correct gauge is important to achieve a good fit.

Note
Instructions for the two larger sizes are given in square brackets, like this: **1st size** [2nd size, **3rd size**].

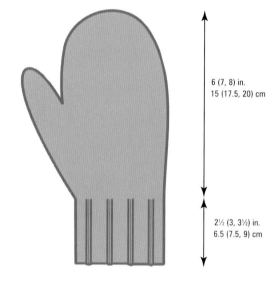

6 (7, 8) in.
15 (17.5, 20) cm

2½ (3, 3½) in.
6.5 (7.5, 9) cm

Making the mitten
(make two)

BEGIN AT WRIST:
Using two of four size US 7 (4.5 mm) double-pointed needles and main yarn, cast on **29** [33, **37**] sts. Arrange sts on three needles: 10 sts / **8** [12, **16**] sts / 11 sts, (ending with first cast-on stitch). Arrange in a triangle without twisting (see pages 24–25), with 11 sts on left-hand needle. Slip first cast-on st from left-hand needle to right-hand needle, lift last cast-on st over it and off needle. **28** [32, **36**] sts, arranged 10 sts / **8** [12, **16**] sts / 10 sts.
Rib round 1: * K2, P2, * repeat from * to * to last 4 sts, K2, P1, place ring marker on right-hand needle, P last st. All rounds begin and end 1 st after this marker. Slip it on every round.
Rib round 2: * K2, P2,* repeat from * to * to end. Repeat round 2 until ribbing measures **2½** [3, **3½**] in. (**6.5** [7.5, **9**] cm), ending 1 st after round marker. Change to stockinette (all rounds knit).
Next round: * K**5** [6, **7**], K2tog, * repeat from * to * three more times. **24** [28, **32**] sts.
Knit **4** [4, **6**] rounds.

SHAPE THUMB

The positions of the thumb increases are marked by two more ring markers. Choose a different color for these, to avoid confusing them with the round marker.

Next round: K**11** [13, **15**], place ring marker, m1tbl, K2, m1tbl, place another ring marker, K**11** [13, **15**] to end of round. **26** [30, **34**] sts.

Knit 1 round.

Inc round: K to first marker, slip marker, m1tbl, K to second marker, m1tbl, slip marker, K to end.

Knit 1 round.

Repeat last 2 rounds **1** [2, **2**] more times. **30** [36, **40**] sts.

Knit **3** [5, **7**] rounds. **13** [17, **21**] stockinette rounds.

Next round: K**12** [14, **16**], slip next **6** [8, **8**] sts onto holder and leave for thumb, cast on **4** [4, **6**] sts by Simple Thumb Cast-on (see page 23), K**12** [14, **16**]. **28** [32, **36**] sts.

Continue in stockinette (all rounds knit) until mitten measures **2** [3, **4**] in. (**5** [7.5, **10**] cm) from sts cast on above thumb opening, ending at round marker.

SHAPE TOP OF MITTEN

As the number of stitches decreases, you will need to slip stitches purlwise (see page 37) from one needle to the next, so that stitches to be worked together are on the same needle.

Round 1: * K1, ssk, K**8** [10, **12**], K2tog, K1, * repeat from * to * once more. **24** [28, **32**] sts.

Round 2: Knit.

Round 3: * K1, ssk, K**6** [8, **10**], K2tog, K1, * repeat from * to * once more. **20** [24, **28**] sts.

Round 4: Knit.

Round 5: * K1, ssk, K**4** [6, **8**], K2tog, K1, * repeat from * to * once more. **16** [20, **24**] sts.

2nd & 3rd sizes only

Round 6: K to end.

Round 7: * K1, ssk, K [4, **6**], K2tog, K1, * repeat from * to * once more. [16, **20**] sts.

3rd size only

Round 8: K to end.

Round 9: * K1, ssk, K4, K2tog, K1, * repeat from * to * once more. 16 sts.

All sizes

16 sts remain.

Next round: * K1, ssk, K2, K2tog, K1, * repeat from * to * once more. 12 sts.

Slip first 6 sts onto another needle. Graft the two sets of sts together (see pages 40–41).

SHAPE THUMB

Using same needles, with right side of work facing, with 1st needle pick up and K**5** [5, **7**] sts from base loops of **4** [4, **6**] sts cast on above thumb opening (see page 55). With 2nd needle, K across first

3 [4, **4**] sts from holder. With 3rd needle, K across remaining **3** [4, **4**] sts from holder (see page 54). **11** [13, **15**] sts.

Knit 1 round, placing ring marker before last st. All rounds begin and end 1 st after this marker.

Work in stockinette (all rounds knit) until thumb measures **1½** [2, **2½**] in. (**3.5** [5, **6**] cm), ending 1 st after marker.

Next round: * K2tog, K**1** [2, **3**], * repeat from * to * twice more, K**2** [1, **0**]. **8** [10, **12**] sts.

Following round: K2tog, **4** [5, **6**] times.

Cut yarn, leaving an 8-in. (20-cm) tail. Thread tail into tapestry needle and slip it through remaining **4** [5, **6**] sts, gathering up tightly in same way as for top of Hat (page 61). Secure firmly, and run in the tail (see page 33).

ASSEMBLY

Run in any remaining yarn tails (see page 33). Block (see page 45).

Our mittens were made in a multi-color tweed yarn, but you can choose any color you would like to suit your winter wardrobe.

See also:

Using Markers (page 31)
Grafting (pages 40–41)
Slipping Stitches (page 37)
Picking Up Stitches (page 54–55)
Abbreviations (page 44)

TIPS

- If necessary, adjust the length of the hand and thumb by working more or fewer rounds before the shaping.
- The hat on pages 68–69 is also in aran-weight yarn, so you could make a hat to match these mittens.

Shaping with darts: decreasing

Decreasing with darts can produce a flat circle, a cone, or a bowl shape, depending on the spacing of the decrease stitches. This type of shaping is used for the Hat (pages 68–69), Cuddly Shoulder Bag (pages 56–57), Bolster Cushion (pages 76–77), and for the yokes on the Family Sweaters (pages 92–97).

You can decrease with darts on a circular needle, but, as the total number of stitches diminishes, you may need to change to a set of double-pointed needles of the same size.

Our example shows shaping the top of a pull-on hat, using double-pointed needles.

Calculating the number of darts

There may be any number of dart sections. The total number of stitches at the base of the shaping must divide evenly by the number of darts required.

In our example, the total number of stitches at the base of the shaping is 96, and we will make six darts of 16 stitches (6 x 16 = 96). Each dart decreases from 16 stitches down to 2, so ending with 6 x 2 = 12 stitches at the top of the hat.

The decrease stitches will form noticeable lines in the finished knitting, so they are carefully arranged to form a pattern. Paired decreases (K2tog followed by Ssk) are used in our example to form neatly defined shaping lines.

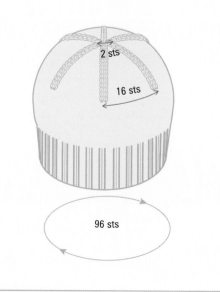

1 Place markers on first decrease round

For six darts, the first decrease round might read: * Ssk, K12, K2tog * repeat from * to * 5 more times. (12 sts decreased.) As you work the first decrease round, place a ring marker at the end of each repeat. As on page 31, the end of each complete round shown here is marked by threading a length of yarn as knitting proceeds.

2 Slip markers on following rounds

Unless you are decreasing very sharply, there will normally be several unshaped rounds between the decrease rounds. Slip each marker as you come to it, and count the complete rounds as you work them.

3 Change to double-pointed needles

As the shaping progresses, there will be fewer stitches and you will probably need to change to a set of double-pointed needles of the same size. Knit one round using the new needles and put the circular needle aside. If you are making six darts, it is convenient to divide the stitches evenly between three double-pointed needles (from a set of four), so there will be two darts on each needle, with a ring marker between each pair of darts. For eight darts, it is easier to use four needles (from a set of five). For other numbers of darts, divide the stitches as evenly as possible between the needles, leaving all the ring markers in place.

5 To finish the top

You can either bind off the last few stitches in the usual way (leaving a small hole), or gather them tightly together, as here. Cut the yarn leaving an 8-in. (20-cm) tail, and thread the tail into a tapestry needle. Slip the needle purlwise through each stitch in turn (see page 37), removing the double-pointed needles and ring markers as you come to them.

6 Gather tightly

Pull tightly on the yarn tail. Pass the needle through the center hole to the inside of the hat.

TIPS

1. Sometimes darts are shaped with the double decrease (see page 39)—for example, * S2togk, K12 * repeat from * to *. (Each dart section decreases from 15 sts to 13.)
2. Working a dart shaping as "Ssk, K2tog" (instead of "K2tog, Ssk") makes a less obvious dart line. See Family Sweaters on pages 92–97.
3. Sometimes a garment design requires shaping at the center of a dart section, so that the shaping lines fall in a different place. For example, * K6, K2tog, Ssk, K6, * gives a similar effect to * Ssk, K12, K2tog *, but the shaping lines will be differently positioned.

4 Complete the decreasing

At the top of this hat, you need to decrease down to just two stitches in each section. (For a sweater yoke, the shaping normally ends with the number of stitches required for the neck border.)

7 Secure the yarn tail

On the inside, make three or four firm backstitches around the center hole, catching the loops of the last round of stitches closely together. Trim the yarn tail, or use it to sew on a tassel or pompon (see pages 100–103).

Short row shaping

In circular knitting, short row shaping is used to add extra rows to just one part of a knitted tube, forming a bend in the tube, as at the heel of a sock. The same technique is used to add extra depth at the back neck of a circular-knit sweater.

A sequence of short rows is worked, each with several stitches less than the row before, until the shaping is complete. To avoid gaps in the knitting, use the Wrapped Stitch technique, shown below.

Short rows and wrapped stitches

Note that the wrapped stitch is always the stitch after the last stitch of the short row. Shown here in stockinette stitch, at the neck opening of a sweater, Steps 1–4 show wrapping a stitch on a knit row, and Steps 6–9 wrapping a stitch on a purl row. The last two photographs (overleaf) show how to work into a wrapped stitch either knitwise or purlwise, hiding the wrap.

1 Knit 1 row, slip one purlwise
Knit the stitches required for the first short row, then slip the next stitch purlwise.

3 Slip to left needle
Insert the left needle tip back into the same stitch from left to right, to prevent twisting, and slip it back onto the left needle.

2 Yarn to front
Bring the yarn to the front of the work, between the needle tips.

4 Yarn to back
Take the yarn through to the back of the work, between the needle tips. The yarn is wrapped around the first stitch on the left needle.

5 Turn work and purl
Turn the work around, so that the purl side is facing you. The yarn is in the correct position to purl the second short row.

8 Slip to left needle
Insert the left needle tip back into the same stitch from left to right, and slip it back onto the left needle. The yarn is wrapped around the first stitch on the left needle.

6 Purl 1 row, slip one purlwise
Purl the number of stitches required for the second short row (usually a few less than for the first row). Slip the next stitch purlwise.

9 Yarn to front
Bring the yarn through to the front of the work, between the needle tips. The yarn is now wrapped around the first stitch on the left needle.

7 Yarn to back
Take the yarn through to the back of the work, between the needle tips.

10 Turn work and knit

Turn the work around so that the knit side is facing you. The yarn is in position for you to knit the next (third) short row.

Knitting a wrapped stitch

After you have completed all the short rows required, the work often continues in rounds. As you knit the next round, you need to hide all the wrapped stitches. When you reach a wrapped stitch, insert the needle under the wrap from the front, and then knitwise into the wrapped stitch. Knit the wrap together with the stitch. The wrap will be hidden, with no gaps between the stitches.

Purling a wrapped stitch

Sometimes you need to purl a wrapped stitch—for example, when beginning a ribbed neckband. Insert the needle from behind, under the wrap, and then purlwise into the wrapped stitch. Purl the wrap together with the stitch.

The wrapped stitches are firm and neat. If you don't wrap the stitches as shown above, small holes will form where the short rows are turned.

TIPS

Sometimes short row shaping is worked with the sequence of rows in reverse—that is, beginning with the shortest row, then working a few more stitches on every subsequent row. In this case, there will be a wrapped stitch near the end of the second and every following row. Work into the wrapped stitches either knitwise or purlwise, as required, as shown on this page.

Project 5: Socks

Circular-knitted socks are super-comfy! They'll keep your feet warm on the coldest of days, and there are no seams to rub your toes. Look for 4-ply (fingering) sock wool, which usually contains a small proportion of synthetic fiber to make it more hardwearing. We chose a multi-colored, "instant fairisle" yarn, which is great fun to knit.

Finished size: To fit foot measured all around at widest part:
7–7½ in. (17.5–19 cm); 8–8½ in. (20–21.5 cm); 9–9½ in. (23–24 cm)

MATERIALS

■ Approx. 4 oz (100 gm) 4-ply sock yarn (230 yards/210 metres to 2 oz/50 gm)

■ Set of four double-pointed needles, size US 3 (3.25 mm), length 8 or 10 in. (20 or 25 cm)

■ Tapestry needle to suit yarn
■ One ring marker

Gauge
30 stitches and 40 rounds to 4 in. (10 cm) measured over stockinette stitch, using size US 3 (3.25 mm) needles. Check gauge as shown on page 42. Correct gauge is important to achieve a good fit.

Note
Instructions for the two larger sizes are given in square brackets, like this:
1st size [2nd size, **3rd size**].

TAKE MEASUREMENTS
Measure all around the foot at the widest part, just below the toes, as shown. Choose the pattern size that most closely matches this measurement (**a**). Measure the length of the foot from the back of the heel to the end of the big toe (**b**). You can knit the foot of the sock to match this length exactly, as instructed below.

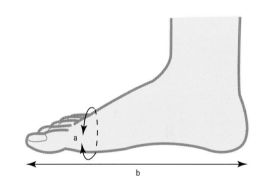

Making the sock
(make two)

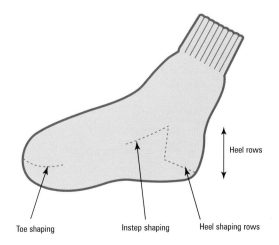

Toe shaping   Instep shaping   Heel shaping rows

Heel rows

BEGIN AT ANKLE

Using two size US 3 (3.25 mm) double-pointed needles, cast on **49** [**57**, **65**] sts. Arrange sts on three needles: **16** [18, **22**] sts / **16** [20, **22**] sts / **17** [19, **21**] sts, ending with first cast-on st. Arrange in a triangle without twisting (see pages 24–25), with **17** [19, **21**] sts on left-hand needle. Slip first cast-on st from left-hand needle to right-hand needle, lift last cast-on st over it and off needle. **48** [**56**, **64**] sts, arranged **16** [18, **22**] sts/ **16** [20, **22**] sts / **16** [18, **20**] sts.

On first round, slip a ring marker onto right-hand needle before working last st. The following rounds begin and end 1 st after this marker, which corresponds to the center back of the leg and heel. Slip the marker on subsequent rounds.

Round 1: * K2, P2, * repeat from * to * to end. Repeat round 1 until work measures **2½** [3, **3½**] in. (**6** [7.5, **8**] cm), ending 1 st after round marker. Change to stockinette stitch (all rounds knit) and work a further **2½** [3, **3½**] in. (**6** [7.5, **8**] cm), ending 1 st after round marker.

SHAPE HEEL

Slip last **12** [14, **16**] sts of previous round onto empty needle, then use this same needle to K first **12** [14, **16**] sts of next round, making **24** [28, **32**] sts on this needle for heel. Arrange remaining **24** [28, **32**] sts evenly on two needles and leave for foot. Work in rows on heel sts:

Heel row 1: Sl1k, P to last st, K1.
Heel row 2: Sl1k, K to end.
Repeat these 2 rows **11** [13, **15**] more times. Work heel row 1 again. **25** [29, **33**] heel rows, ending P row.

Next row: Sl1k, K**12** [14, **16**], K2tog, K1, turn leaving **8** [10, **12**] sts unworked.
Following row: Sl1p, P3, P2tog, P1, turn leaving **8** [10, **12**] sts unworked.
Following row: Sl1k, K4, K2tog, K1, turn leaving **6** [8, **10**] sts unworked.
Following row: Sl1p, P5, P2tog, P1, turn leaving **6** [8, **10**] sts unworked.
Continue in this way, working 1 extra st on each row before working two together, until all sts have been worked, ending P row. **14** [16, **18**] sts remain.
Continue in rounds:
Next round: 1st needle: K**14** [16, **18**] sts, then pick up and K**14** [16, **18**] sts down side edge of heel rows. 2nd needle: K across all **24** [28, **32**] sts from two needles left for foot, onto one needle. 3rd needle: Pick up and K**14** [16, **18**] sts from side edge of heel rows, then slip first **7** [8, **9**] sts of round from 1st needle onto empty needle and K them onto 3rd needle. **66** [76, **86**] sts, arranged **21** [24, **27**] sts / **24** [28, **32**] sts / **21** [24, **27**] sts, ending 1 st after round marker.
Knit 3 rounds.

SHAPE INSTEP

Instep dec round: 1st needle: K to last 3 sts, K2tog, K1. 2nd needle: K across all sts. 3rd needle: K1, ssk, K to end. **64** [74, **84**] sts.
Knit 2 rounds.
Repeat these 3 rounds **8** [9, **10**] more times. **48** [56, **64**] sts.
Work without shaping until foot measures **6** [6½, **7**] in. (**15** [16.5, **17.5**] cm). Adjust foot length here: foot of sock should measure **2** [2½, **3**] in. (**5** [6, **7.5**] cm) less than measurement **b**, measured from center of heel shaping at back of heel.

Using multi-color "instant fairisle" yarn adds interest to these classic socks. They are knitted from the top of the ankle down to the toe.

SHAPE TOE

Toe round 1: 1st needle: K to last 3 sts, K2tog, K1. 2nd needle: K1, ssk, K to last 3 sts, K2tog, K1. 3rd needle: K1, ssk, K to end. **44** [52, **60**] sts.
Knit 2 rounds.
Repeat these three rounds **5** [6, **7**] more times. **24** [28, **32**] sts.
Repeat Toe Round twice more, ending 1 st after round marker. **16** [20, **24**] sts, arranged **4** [5, **6**] sts / **8** [10, **12**] sts / **4** [5, **6**] sts.
K first **4** [5, **6**] sts of next round, then slip **4** [5, **6**] sts from 3rd needle onto the right-hand end of this needle, making **8** [10, **12**] sts on each of two needles, with working yarn end between needles. Cut yarn, leaving a 12-in. (30-cm) tail, and use tapestry needle to graft toe (see pages 40–41). Run in any remaining yarn tails (see page 33).

The socks are perfect for lounging indoors, or to keep your toes warm in winter boots.

TIPS

- You can try on the sock to test the foot length: knit to halfway along the second needle, spread the stitches out along the needles (but not too close to the tips), and slip the sock onto your foot.
- When using instant fairisle yarn, make the second sock match the first by winding off a little yarn from the ball so that you can begin at the same point in the color sequence.

See also:
Using Markers (page 31)
Slipping Stitches Knitwise and Purlwise (page 37)
Picking Up Stitches (pages 54–55)
Abbreviations (page 44)

Project 6: Hat

This cozy hat is quick to knit, using both circular and double-pointed needles. The same weight of yarn is used for the Mittens on paged 58–59, so you could make a matching set.

Finished size: To fit head sizes: 19–20 in. (48–51 cm); 21–22 in. (53–56 cm); 23–24 in. (58.5–61 cm)

MATERIALS

- Approx. 4 oz (100 gm) aran-weight yarn (approx. 100 yds/90 metres to 2 oz/50 gm)
- Circular needle, size US 7 (4.5 mm), length 16 in. (40 cm)
- Circular needle, size US 8 (5mm), length 16 in. (40 cm)
- Set of four double-pointed needles, size US 8 (5mm), length 8 in. (20 cm)
- One thread marker, five ring markers
- Tapestry needle to suit yarn

Gauge
18 stitches and 24 rounds to 4 in. (10 cm) measured over stockinette stitch using size US 8 (5 mm) needles. Check gauge as shown on page 42. Correct gauge is important for a good fit.

Note
Instructions for the different sizes are given in square brackets, like this: **1st size** [2nd size, **3rd size**].

Making the hat

Using a circular needle size US 7 (4.5 mm), cast on **85** [97, **109**] sts. Arrange sts in a circle without twisting (see page 24), with last cast-on st on right-hand needle. Slip first cast-on st from left-hand needle to right-hand needle, lift last cast-on st over it and off needle. **84** [96, **108**] sts. Place a thread marker (see page 31) on right-hand needle. All rounds begin and end at this marker.

Round 1: * K2, P2, * repeat from * to * to end. Repeat this round until work measures **2** [2½, **3**] in. (**5** [6.5, **7.5**] cm), ending at thread marker.

Change to a size US 8 (5 mm) circular needle and stockinette stitch (all rounds knit).

Knit until work measures **4** [5, **6**] in. (**10** [12.5, **15**] cm), ending at thread marker.

SHAPE TOP OF HAT

The top of the hat is shaped in six darts, as shown on pages 60–61.

As the number of stitches decreases, you will need to change to a set of four size US 8 (5 mm) double-pointed needles.

On the next round, place five ring markers, to mark the positions of the decreases:

Next round: Slip thread marker, * K2tog, K**10** [12, **14**], ssk, place ring marker, * repeat from * to * five more times ending last repeat at thread marker. **72** [84, **96**] sts.

Knit 3 rounds, slipping all markers.

Dec round: Slip thread marker, * K2tog, K to 2 sts before marker, ssk, slip ring marker, * repeat from * to * to end. **60** [72, **84**] sts.

Knit 3 rounds.

See also:
Using Markers (page 31)
Abbreviations (page 44)
Tassels (pages 100–101)

Repeat last 4 rounds **1** [1, **2**] more times. **48** [60, **60**] sts.

Repeat dec round.

Knit 1 round. **36** [48, **48**] sts.

Repeat these 2 rounds **2** [3, **3**] more times. 12 sts remain.

Cut yarn, leaving an 8-in. (20-cm) tail. Thread tail into tapestry needle and gather up remaining 12 sts as shown on page 61, removing markers.

ASSEMBLY

Run in any remaining yarn tails (see page 33). Make a tassel (see pages 100–101) and sew it to the top of the hat. Block (see page 45).

This close-fitting hat is shaped with darts and finished with a matching tassel.

TIPS

- If you prefer, you can use double-pointed needles throughout for this project.
- Instead of a tassel, add a pompon as shown on pages 102–103.
- Add a band of two-color fairisle patterning to the unshaped rounds between the ribbing and the shaping. Any fairisle pattern requiring a stitch multiple of 4, 6, or 12 stitches will be suitable.

Textured stitch techniques

In circular knitting, textured stitches such as twists, cables, and
bobbles are made using the same methods as in row-by-row knitting.

Twists

Twists are pairs of stitches worked out of
order, the second stitch before the first. No
cable needle is required. There are several
methods for working both left and right
twists, but the two techniques described
here give the neatest effect.

Left twist (Tw2L)

By knitting the second stitch behind the first,
the twist that forms slopes up to the left.

2 Knit both stitches together through back loops

Now insert the right needle through
the first and second stitches together,
from right to left, and draw through
another loop.

1 Knit second stitch through back loop
Work to the required position. Insert the right
needle tip through the back of the second stitch
from right to left, and draw through a loop in the
usual way, leaving the stitch on the left needle.

Drop both stitches from left needle
Allow both stitches to drop from the left needle, and
continue the round. Moving the position of the twist by
one stitch to the left on every alternate round creates a
diagonal line sloping up to the left, as here.

Right twist (Tw2R)

There are two or three ways to form a twist sloping up to the right, but this method gives the neatest result.

1 Knit two together

Work to where the twist is required. Insert the right needle knitwise through the next two stitches together (as for Knit Two Together, see page 38), and draw through a loop in the usual way, without slipping the stitches off the left needle.

3 Drop stitches from left needle

Allow both stitches to drop from the left needle, and continue the round. Moving the position of the twist by one stitch to the right on every alternate round creates a diagonal line sloping up to the right, as here.

2 Knit first stitch again

Knit the first stitch again in the usual way.

TIPS

- By twisting the same pair of stitches on every alternate round, a tiny two-stitch cable is formed, here bordered by a purl stitch on each side.
- For more twist stitch patterns, see page 114.
- By twisting stitches on every round (instead of on every alternate round), the diagonal lines can be made to slope at a different angle.

Cables

Cables are made by slipping a small group of stitches to a cable needle, working the next group, and then working the group from the cable needle. The cable needle may be held at the front or the back of the work, creating a twist to the left or a twist to the right.

A cable needle is a double-pointed needle about 4 in. (10 cm) long, which may be straight or "cranked" to hold the slipped stitches more securely (see page 13). Choose a cable needle one or two sizes smaller than those you are knitting with, to prevent stretching the slipped stitches. A 6-in. (15-cm) double-pointed needle can be used as a substitute.

Cable twisted to the left (C6L or C6F)

This six-stitch cable is shown on a background of reverse stockinette stitch. The stitches forming the cable itself are worked in stockinette stitch.

1 Slip to cable needle
Work to where the cable is required, and slip the first group of stitches purlwise onto the cable needle (three stitches are shown here).

The cable twists to the left. Here, cables have been worked on every sixth round.

Cable twisted to the right (C6R or C6B)

This six-stitch cable is also shown on a background of reverse stockinette stitch.

Hold at back
Work as above, but at Step 2 hold the cable needle at the back of the work while you work the second group of stitches.

2 Hold at front
Hold the cable needle at the front of the work, and knit the second group of (three) stitches.

The cable twists to the right. Here, cables have been worked on every sixth round.

3 Knit from cable needle
Then knit the stitches from the cable needle, and continue the round.

TIPS

- For cable stitch patterns, see pages 112–113.
- Cables may be many sizes, from two or four stitches wide up to about ten or twelve stitches.
- Combinations of right and left cables, together with knit or purl stitches produce variations.
- Cables may also be bordered by just one or two purl stitches which helps the cables to stand out clearly in relief.

Bobbles

Bobbles are made by working several times into one stitch, then decreasing back to one stitch again before continuing the round. Larger bobbles may be formed by increasing the number of stitches made, and working one or two rows on them, before decreasing back to one stitch. However, turning circular knitting to work the extra rows can be clumsy, so smaller bobbles are much easier for circular knitting.

Make a small bobble (MSB)

This method of making a bobble forms a small, firm "ball" on the surface of the knitting.

1 Knit three times into one stitch
Work to where the bobble is required, then knit into the front (insert left to right), back (insert right to left), and front again of the next stitch, making three stitches on the right needle.

2 Pass stitches over
Use the left needle tip to lift the second stitch over the third, and off the right needle. Then lift the first stitch over and off, in the same way.

Purl bobble (PB)

This bobble is looser and flatter than the small bobble shown above, resembling a tiny flower.

1 Purl three together
Work to where the bobble is required. Purl the next three stitches together, leaving them on the left needle.

2 Yarn over
Take the yarn over the top of the right needle, and bring it to the front between the needle tips, making an extra stitch.

3 Push to front
Pull firmly on the yarn, and make sure that the bobble lies at the front of the work as you continue the round. The bobble should stand out from the surface of the knitting.

See Also

• Gloves (variation) **p80**

3 Purl three together again
Purl the same three stitches together again, allowing them to slip from the left needle.

4 Push to front
Pull the yarn firmly and make sure that the bobble is at the front of the work as you continue the round.

Project 7: Two pillows

By shaping circular knitting in various ways, you can create simple geometric shapes such as squares, circles, and tubes. Try out these shaping techniques by making these colorful pillows: the first is made from two squares, the second is a tube with a circle at each end.

Finished size: To fit 14 in. (35 cm) square pillow form

MATERIALS

■ Approx. 4 oz (100 gm) bulky yarn (approx. 109 yds/100 metres to 4 oz/100 gm) in each of 3 colors, A, B, and C
■ Small ball of waste yarn

■ Circular needle, size US 10½ (7 mm), length 24 in. (60 cm)
■ Set of five double-pointed needles, size US 10½ (7 mm), length 8 in. (20 cm)

■ One ring marker in color A, three ring markers in color B
■ Tapestry needle to suit yarn
■ 14-in. (35-cm) square polyester fiber-filled pillow form

Gauge

12 stitches and 17 rounds to 4 in. (10 cm) measured over stockinette stitch, using size US 10½ (7 mm) needles. Gauge is not crucial provided a change in size is acceptable, but if the gauge is too loose, the filling may show through the knitting, and extra yarn may be required.

See also:
Provisional Cast-on (page 52)
Using Markers (page 31)
Running In Tails (page 33)
Picking Up Stitches (pages 54–55)
Abbreviations (page 44)

Square pillow

By shaping the knitting with four darts, decreasing sharply, a flat square is formed. Two such squares make this cozy pillow, knitted in bulky yarn. Choose any three colors to suit your room.

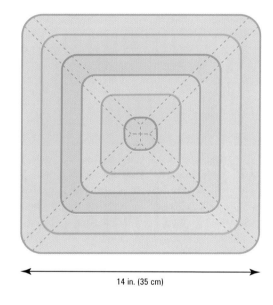

14 in. (35 cm)

FIRST SQUARE

The square is knitted from the outside edge in toward the center.

Begin with a provisional cast-on (see page 52): using a size US 10½ (7 mm) circular needle and waste yarn, cast on 192 sts. Arrange in a circle without twisting (see page 24).

Use ring markers of one color for the dart markers, and a ring marker of another color for the last (round) marker:

Preparation round: K46, * place a dart marker, K48, * repeat from * to * twice more, place last (round) marker, K2. All rounds begin and end 2 sts after the last (round) marker. Slip all the markers on every following round.

Change to color A.

Round 1: K to end.

Round 2: * K to 3 sts before marker, K2tog, K1, slip marker, K1, ssk, * repeat from * to * three more times. 184 sts.

Round 3: Repeat round 2. 176 sts.

Rounds 4–6: Repeat rounds 1–3. 160 sts.

Cut color A, leaving a 6-in. (15-cm) tail. Join in color B.

Rounds 7–12: Repeat rounds 1–6. 128 sts.

Cut color B, leaving a 6-in. (15-cm) tail. Join in color C.

Rounds 13–18: Repeat rounds 1–6. 96 sts.

At some point, you will need to change to a set of five size US 10½ (7 mm) double-pointed needles, because the circular needle will be too long for the number of stitches. Knit one-quarter of the sts onto each of four needles, removing the dart markers, and replace the round marker with a thread marker (see page 31).

Cut color C, leaving a 6-in. (15-cm) tail. Join in color A.

Repeat rounds 1–6. 64 sts.

Cut color A, leaving a 6-in. (15-cm) tail. Join in color B.

Repeat rounds 1–6. 32 sts.

Cut color B, leaving a 6-in. (15-cm) tail. Join in color C.

Repeat rounds 1–3 only. 16 sts.

Knit 1 round. Cut color C, leaving an 8-in. (20-cm) tail, and thread the tail into a tapestry needle. Slip the needle through the remaining sts and gather the center of the pillow tightly, in the same way as the top of the Hat, on page 61.

SECOND SQUARE

In order to use only 4 oz (100 gm) of each color, you need to knit the second square using the colors in reverse order.

Work as for First Square, but with stripe sequence C, B, A.

ASSEMBLY

Run in all the yarn tails (see page 33).

Place the two squares wrong sides together, matching the corner darts exactly. Fold the waste yarn edges back toward the center of each side, so that you can see the loops of the first round in A on one square and the first round in C on the other square.

BIND-OFF SEAM

Begin at one corner: insert one double-pointed needle through two corresponding loops (one from each square), and use color B to form a stitch (see page 52). * Pick up another stitch from next two

corresponding loops, then use a second double-pointed needle to bind off 1 st.* Repeat from * to * all around three sides of the pillow.

Run in the yarn tail left at the start of the seam. Insert the pillow form, then complete the fourth side in the same way.

Remove the waste yarn (see page 52).

Run in remaining yarn tail from the right side.

The clever shaping on this square pillow makes a bold, geometric design.

TIPS

- Knit the pillow in random stripes, changing colors as often as you wish.
- A polyester fiber-filled pillow form need not be removed for washing. Wash the pillow by hand (in a similar way to blocking, page 45) and leave in a warm, airy place to dry completely.

Finished size: Length 15 in. (38 cm), diameter 8½ in. (21.5 cm)

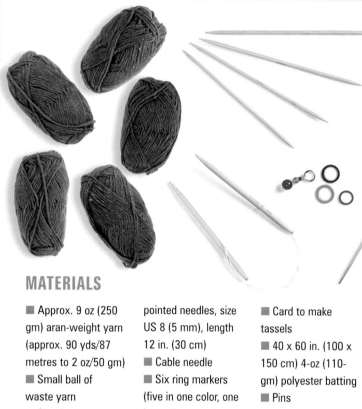

MATERIALS

- Approx. 9 oz (250 gm) aran-weight yarn (approx. 90 yds/87 metres to 2 oz/50 gm)
- Small ball of waste yarn
- Circular needle, size US 8 (5 mm), length 16 in. (40 cm)
- Set of four double-pointed needles, size US 8 (5 mm), length 12 in. (30 cm)
- Cable needle
- Six ring markers (five in one color, one in another color)
- Tapestry needle to suit yarn
- Card to make tassels
- 40 x 60 in. (100 x 150 cm) 4-oz (110-gm) polyester batting
- Pins
- Sharp sewing needle and white sewing thread

Gauge
18 stitches and 24 rounds to 4 in. (10 cm) measured over stockinette stitch, using size US 8 (5 mm) needles. Gauge is not crucial provided a change in size is acceptable, but if the gauge is too loose, the filling may show through the knitting, and extra yarn may be required.

Bolster pillow

This tube-shaped pillow is quick and fun to knit. Make two or three in different colors to brighten up your sofa! This pattern is very adaptable, so you could try out some different stitch patterns (see Tip, opposite).

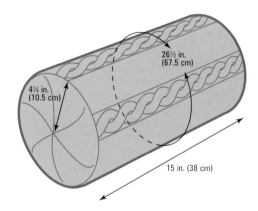

26½ in. (67.5 cm)
4¼ in. (10.5 cm)
15 in. (38 cm)

MAKING THE TUBULAR PART OF THE PILLOW

Begin with a provisional cast-on (see page 52): using a size US 8 (5 mm) circular needle and waste yarn, cast on 120 sts. Arrange in a circle without twisting (see page 24). Slip ring marker onto right-hand needle tip. All rounds begin and end at this marker. Slip it at the beginning of every round.
Knit 1 round, ending at marker.
Change to main yarn.
Knit 1 round.

Cable Pattern:
Round 1: * K6, P1, K6, P1, K6, * repeat from * to * five more times, ending at round marker.
Rounds 2–4: Repeat round 1.
Round 5: * K6, P1, C6L, P1, K6, * repeat from * to * five more times.
Rounds 6–8: Repeat round 1.
These 8 rounds form the cable pattern. Repeat them until work measures 15 in. (38 cm) from first round in main yarn, ending round 8.
Knit 1 round.

See also:
Provisional Cast-on (page 52)
Using Markers (page 31)
Cable Stitches (page 72)
Picking Up Stitches (page 54–55)
Abbreviations (page 44)

FIRST CIRCLE

The circle is shaped with six darts, in a similar way to the top of the hat on pages 60–61, but because the decreasing rounds are close together, a flat circle is formed.

** Purl 1 round.

Use a different color for the new markers:

1st dec round: * Ssk, K18, place a ring marker, * repeat from * to * five more times ending at round marker.

2nd dec round: * Ssk, K to next marker, slip marker, * repeat from * to * five more times.

3rd dec round: Repeat 2nd dec round.

4th dec round: K to end, slipping all markers.

5th dec round: Repeat 2nd dec round.

Repeat 2nd to 5th rounds until 12 stitches remain. (After a few rounds, you will need to change to the set of size US 8 (5 mm) double-pointed needles, because the circular needle will be too long for the number of sts.) At this point, you can substitute a thread marker for the round marker.

Next round: Ssk, six times. 6 sts remain.

Cut yarn, leaving an 8-in. (20-cm) tail. Thread tail into tapestry needle and slip it through remaining 6 sts, gathering tightly in same way as top of the hat on page 61. Fasten off securely and run in tail.

ASSEMBLY

Turn work wrong side out and run in all the tails (see page 33). Turn right side out.

Cut batting into four 40 x 15-in. (100 x 38-cm) strips. Stack three strips and roll them up tightly, then wrap the fourth strip around the outside, pinning the edge in place. Use needle and thread to catch down the free edge of the batting with large zigzag stitches, as shown.

Insert the batting tube into the bolster and push it down hard, away from the open end.

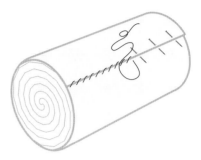

SECOND CIRCLE

With right side of work facing, using circular needle size US 8 (5 mm) and main yarn, pick up and K 120 sts from loops of first round in main color, as shown on page 52. Place a ring marker on right needle tip.

Work as First Circle from ** to end.

TRIM

Use main yarn to make two tassels about 3 in. (7.5 cm) long (see pages 100–101) and sew one at the center of each circular end.

This bolster-shaped pillow is made from a tube with a flat, darted circle at each end, trimmed with tassels.

TIPS

- Many stitch patterns from the Stitch Library may be substituted for the cable pattern on the tubular part of the bolster. For the tube, you need 120 sts, so any pattern requiring a multiple of 3, 4, 5, 6, 8, 10, or 12 sts would be suitable. Ribs, other cables, textured stitches, and fairisle patterns would all work well, but lace patterns with holes are not suitable because the filling would show through the lacy holes.

- You could also knit the tubular part of the bolster in stripes (see pages 32–33).

- The filling described need not be removed for washing. Wash the bolster by hand (in a similar way to blocking, page 45) and leave in a warm, airy place to dry completely.

Project 8: Gloves

Traditional gloves with closely-fitting fingers are knitted on double-pointed needles for a comfortable, seam-free fit. The circular knit construction is fascinating to work, and you can adjust the lengths of the fingers and thumb to suit any hand. Choose pure wool yarn for its elasticity and warmth.

Finished size: To fit hand measured all around at knuckles: 6½–7¼ in. (16.5–18.5 cm); 7½–8¼ in. (19–21 cm); 8½–9¼ in. (21.5–23.5 cm)

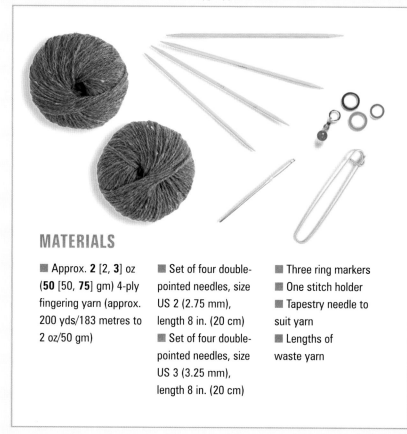

MATERIALS

- Approx. **2** [2, **3**] oz (**50** [50, **75**] gm) 4-ply fingering yarn (approx. 200 yds/183 metres to 2 oz/50 gm)
- Set of four double-pointed needles, size US 2 (2.75 mm), length 8 in. (20 cm)
- Set of four double-pointed needles, size US 3 (3.25 mm), length 8 in. (20 cm)
- Three ring markers
- One stitch holder
- Tapestry needle to suit yarn
- Lengths of waste yarn

Gauge
30 stitches and 40 rounds to 4 in. (10 cm) measured over stockinette stitch, using size US 3 (3.25 mm) needles. Check gauge as shown on page 42. Correct gauge is important to achieve a good fit.

Note
Instructions for the two larger sizes are given in square brackets, like this: **1st size** [2nd size, **3rd size**].

Making the glove
(make two)
Begin at wrist:

Using two of four size US 2 (2.75 mm) double-pointed needles, cast on **49** [57, **65**] sts. Arrange sts on three needles: **16** [18, **22**] sts / **16** [20, **22**] sts/ **17** [19, **21**] sts, (ending with first cast-on stitch). Arrange in a triangle without twisting (see pages 24–25), with **17** [19, **21**] sts on left-hand needle. Slip first cast-on st from left-hand needle to right-hand needle, lift last cast-on st over it and off needle. **48** [56, **64**] sts, arranged **16** [18, **22**] sts / **16** [20, **22**] sts/ **16** [18, **20**] sts.

On first round, place ring marker on right-hand needle before last stitch. All rounds begin and end 1 st after this marker, which corresponds to the outside edge of the hand in line with the little finger. Slip the round marker on every subsequent round.

Rib round: * K2, P2, * repeat from * to * to end. Repeat this round until ribbing measures **2** [2½, **3**] in. (**5** [6.5, **7.5**] cm), ending 1 st after round marker.

Change to stockinette stitch (all rounds knit) and size US 3 (3.25 mm) needles.

Knit 3 rounds.

TAKE MEASUREMENTS

Measure the hand around the knuckles, as shown. Choose the pattern size that most closely matches this measurement.

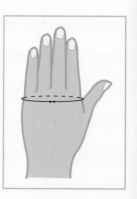

The 4-ply tweed, woolen yarn used for these gloves is soft and warm yet also springy, so it knits up quite firmly for a snug fit.

SHAPE THUMB

Use ring markers of another color to mark the position of the thumb increases:

Next round: K**22** [26, **30**], place thumb marker, m1tbl, K4, m1tbl, place thumb marker, K**22** [26, **30**] to end. **50** [58, **66**] sts.

Knit 3 rounds, slipping all markers.

Inc round: K to thumb marker, slip marker, m1tbl, K to next thumb marker, m1tbl, slip marker, K to end. **52** [60, **68**] sts.

Repeat last 4 rounds, **2** [3, **4**] more times. **56** [66, **76**] sts, with **12** [14, **16**] sts between thumb markers.

Continue in rounds, slipping all markers, until length from last row of ribbing measures **1¾** [2¼, **2¾**] in. (**4.5** [5.5, **7**] cm), or ¼ in. (5 mm) less than measurement **a**, ending 1 st after round marker.

Next round: K to thumb marker, remove marker, slip next **12** [14, **16**] sts to stitch holder, cast on 6 sts by Simple Thumb Cast-on method (see page 23), remove next marker, K to end, slipping round marker. **50** [58, **66**] sts. Arrange in a triangle.

Next round: K to end, slipping round marker. Continue in rounds on these sts until work measures **3** [3½, **4**] in. (**7.5** [9, **10**] cm) from end of ribbing, or to match measurement **b**, ending 1 st after round marker.

TIPS

- You can try on the glove to test the fit as work proceeds: knit to halfway along the second needle, spread out the stitches on the needles, keeping them away from the tips, and slip your hand inside.
- When knitting up stitches for fingers from length of yarn, leave the length of yarn in place until you have knitted all the fingers and made the second glove to match. That way, you can easily count the rounds above the length of yarn to make the second set of fingers exactly the same length.
- Try knitting the main part in stripes, and use a different color for each finger!

The lengths of the various parts of the gloves may be adjusted to fit exactly. Measure the lengths required for each part, as follows, and write them down:

a narrowest part of wrist to base of thumb

b narrowest part of wrist to base of first finger

c length of first finger

d length of second finger

e length of third finger

f length of fourth finger

g length of thumb

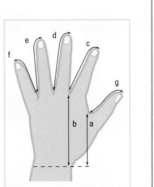

ARRANGE STS FOR FINGERS

K**33** [**38**, **43**], use tapestry needle to slip remaining **17** [20, **23**] sts onto a length of waste yarn, removing round marker. Slip next **17** [20, **23**] sts onto same length of yarn, leaving **16** [18, **20**] sts in work. Slip these sts onto one needle.

FIRST FINGER

Slip first **6** [7, **8**] sts onto a 2nd needle and next **6** [7, **8**] sts onto a 3rd needle, leaving 2 sts on 1st needle, ending at yarn tail. Cast 3 sts onto this needle using Simple Thumb Cast-on method (see page 23), making **19** [21, **23**] sts. Arrange these sts on three needles as evenly as possible.

Next round: K to end, placing marker before last st.

Continue in rounds until finger measures **2¼** [2½, **2¾**] in. (**6** [6.5, **7**] cm), or ¼ in. (5 mm) less than measurement **c**, ending 1 st after marker.

Shape top of first finger

Next round: * K2tog, K2 [2, **1**], * repeat from * to * **3** [3, **5**] more times, K2tog, K**1** [3, **3**]. **14** [16, **16**] sts. Knit 1 round.

Last round: K2tog, **7** [8, **8**] times, removing marker. Cut yarn, leaving an 8-in. (20-cm) tail, and thread tail into tapestry needle. Put one finger inside the glove finger and thread the tail through remaining **7** [8, **8**] sts, gathering tightly and securing in same way as for top of Hat, page 61.

SECOND FINGER

With right side of work facing, on 1st needle pick up and K 4 sts from base loops of 3 cast-on sts at base of first finger. With 2nd needle, K up first **6** [7, **8**] sts from length of yarn, then cast on 3 sts as before. With 3rd needle, K up last **6** [7, **8**] sts from length of yarn. **19** [21, **23**] sts. Arrange these sts on three needles as evenly as possible.

Next round: K to end, placing marker before last st.

Continue in rounds until finger measures **2½** [2¾, **3**] in. (**6.5** [7, **7.5**] cm), or ¼ in. (5 mm) less than measurement **d**, ending 1 st after marker.
Shape top of second finger as for first finger.

THIRD FINGER

With right side of work facing, on 1st needle pick up and K 4 sts from base loops of 3 cast-on sts at base of second finger. With 2nd needle, K up next **5** [6, **7**] sts from length of yarn, then cast on 2 sts as before. With 3rd needle, K up last **5** [6, **7**] sts from length of yarn. **16** [18, **20**] sts. Arrange these sts on three needles as evenly as possible.

Next round: K to end, placing marker before last st.

Continue in rounds until finger measures **2¼** [2½, **2¾**] in. (**6** [6.5, **7**] cm), or ¼ in. (5 mm) less than measurement **e**, ending 1 st after marker.

Shape top of third finger

Next round: * K2tog, K2 [1, **1**], * repeat from * to * **2** [4, **4**] more times, K2tog, K**2** [1, **3**]. **12** [12, **14**] sts. Knit 1 round.

Last round: K2tog, **6** [6, **7**] times removing marker. Gather up remaining **6** [6, **7**] sts and secure as for first finger.

FOURTH FINGER

With right side of work facing, on 1st needle pick up and K 3 sts from base loops of 2 cast-on sts at base of third finger. With 2nd needle, K up next **6** [7, **8**] sts from length of yarn. With 3rd needle, K up remaining **6** [7, **8**] sts from length of yarn. **15** [17, **19**] sts. Arrange these sts on three needles as evenly as possible.

Next round: K to end, placing marker before last st.

Continue in rounds until finger measures **1¾** [2, **2¼**] in. (**4.5** [5, **5.5**] cm), or ¼ in. (5 mm) less than measurement **f**, ending 1 st after marker.

Shape top of fourth finger

Next round: * K2tog, K**1** [1, **2**], * repeat from * to * three more times, K2tog, K**1** [3, **1**]. **10** [12, **14**] sts. Knit 1 round.

Last round: K2tog, **5** [6, **7**] times (removing marker). Gather up remaining **5** [6, **7**] sts and secure as for first finger.

THUMB

With right side of work facing, with 1st needle pick up and K 7 sts from base loops of 6 cast-on sts at top of thumb opening. With 2nd needle K first **6** [7, **8**] sts from holder. With 3rd needle K remaining **6** [7, **8**] sts from holder. **19** [21, **23**] sts. Arrange these sts on three needles as evenly as possible.

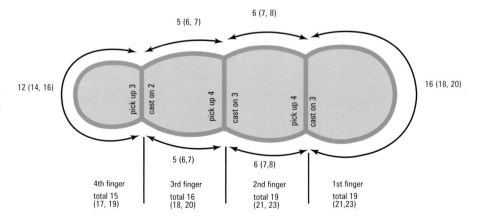

Next round: K to end, placing marker before last st.
Continue in rounds until thumb measures **2** [2¼, **2½**] in. (**5** [5.5, **6**] cm), or ¼ in. (5 mm) less than measurement **g**, ending 1 st after marker. Shape top of thumb as for first finger.

ASSEMBLY
Run in any remaining yarn tails (see page 33). Block (see page 45).

Cable panel gloves
Add a panel of cables and bobbles to the plain version of the gloves.
You will need the same materials as for the plain gloves, plus a small cable needle, and two extra ring markers.
MSB = make small bobble (see page 73)

Cable and Bobble Panel (14 sts wide)
Rounds 1, 2, & 3: P2, K1, P1, K6, P1, K1, P2.
Round 4: P2, MSB, P1, C6R, P1, MSB, P2.
Rounds 5, 6 & 7: as round 1.
Round 8: P2, MSB, P1, K6, P1, MSB, P2.
Repeat these 8 rounds.

RIGHT GLOVE
Cast on as for the plain glove, then position the Cable and Bobble Panel as follows:

1st size only
Rib round 1: K1, P2, K2, place ring marker, work 14 sts as round 1 of panel, place ring marker, * K2, P2, * repeat from * to * to last st, K1.

2nd size only
Rib round 1: P1, K2, P2, K2, place ring marker, work 14 sts as round 1 of panel, place ring marker, * K2, P2, * repeat from * to * to last 3 sts, K2, P1.

3rd size only
Rib round 1: K1, [P2, K2] twice, place ring marker, work 14 sts as round 1 of panel, place ring marker, * K2, P2, * repeat from * to * to last st, K1.

All sizes
Continue as for plain glove, keeping the panel in position as set up to the base of the fingers, repeating the 8 panel rounds as required. Then complete the fingers and thumb as for plain glove, removing the extra ring markers.

LEFT GLOVE
Work to match Right Glove, working C6L instead of C6R, and positioning the Cable and Bobble Panel as follows:

1st size only
Rib round 1: K1, [P2, K2] 7 times, place ring marker, work 14 sts as round 1 of panel, place ring marker, K2, P2, K1.

2nd size only
Rib round 1: P1, K2, [P2, K2] 8 times, place ring marker, work 14 sts as round 1 of panel, place ring marker, K2, P2, K2, P1.

3rd size only
Rib round 1: K1, [P2, K2] 10 times, place ring marker, work 14 sts as round 1 of panel, place ring marker, [K2, P2] twice, K1.

Choose a plain 4-ply yarn for this variation on the basic glove pattern, with a cable panel running along the back of each hand.

See also:
Using Markers (page 31)
Using Stitch Holders (page 53)
Picking Up Stitches (pages 54–55)
Simple Thumb Cast-on (page 23)
MSB (page 73)
Abbreviations (page 44)

Color work techniques

Fairisle or two-color knitting is easy in circular knitting, because the right side is always facing you, so you can see exactly where you are in the pattern.

It is usual to knit with no more than two colors in any one round, otherwise the knitting becomes rather bulky. As the colors are changed, "floats" form on the wrong side of the work; that is, the color not in use is carried loosely across the back of the work to where it is next required. Such floats should be no longer than five stitches. Patterns with longer floats are not included in this book.

Suitable yarns and needles

Soft, elastic yarns that are not too tightly twisted "sit together" well in color knitting, making an even surface with no gaps. Lightly spun wool is the traditional choice. It is more difficult to achieve a neat result with smooth or firmly twisted yarns such as tightly spun cottons or wools.

Many knitters find that to match the gauge of color knitting to that of stockinette stitch, they need to use needles one (or two) sizes larger.

Stranding

Use this technique to carry a color behind one, two, three, or four stitches. Suitable stitch patterns are numbers 1 to 9 on pages 122–123.

Shown here is the two-handed method of stranding. It may seem awkward at first, but with practice it becomes second nature, and the work proceeds both quickly and neatly.

1 Hold one color in each hand

Wind one color (A) around the fingers of your right hand, as for Scottish (or English) knitting, page 18, and the other color (B) around your left hand, as for German (or Continental) knitting, page 18. If one color is used more than the other, hold this color in your right hand.

2 Knit from either hand as required

Knit stitches in color A as for the Scottish (or English) method, and stitches in color B as for the German (or Continental) method (see page 26). Do not pull the yarns too tightly. Keep the new stitches on the right-hand needle spread out, so that the strands of yarn across the back are not too short.

3 Wrong side

The colors will automatically be correctly stranded: on the wrong side, color A is "above", and color B is "below", all along the round. Correct stranding makes for a neat appearance on the right side of the work.

Reading from charts

This chart is 12 stitches wide, so the number of stitches on the needle(s) must divide exactly by 12. The chart rows are numbered on the right, from bottom to top. In circular knitting, all chart rows are read from right to left.

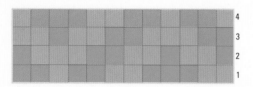

Each square represents one stitch. Begin at bottom right. Row 1 reads "K 2 blue, 3 orange, 2 blue, 2 orange, 1 blue, 2 orange." You should then repeat these 12 stitches as required to complete the round.

Work each round in turn, repeating them as required.

Traveling lines

This technique lends itself well to circular knitting. One ball of the main color (A) is used throughout. Quite short lengths of contrasting colors are required, so they are easy to untangle from time to time. The lines shown here are one stitch wide, but two-stitch widths are also possible (requiring twice as much yarn). See pages 122–123 for more patterns.

1 Join B where required

Knit in the main color (A) to the point where the contrasting color is required. Estimate the total length of the traveling line and cut a length of contrast color (B) three times as long. Knot one end of B around A close to the work, leaving a tail to run in later.

2 Knit with B

Bring B up from behind A, and knit the next stitch.

3 Drop B and pick up A from

behind B, so that it crosses over the top of B. Continue knitting the round. You can join in more traveling lines at intervals on the same round.

4 Travel to the right

To move the line to the right, knit all around to one stitch before the stitch in B, and repeat Steps 2 and 3.

5 Travel to the left

To move the line to the left, knit all around, then use A to knit the B stitch. Repeat Steps 2 and 3 on the next stitch. In this example, the contrasting stitch is moved to the left on every alternate round, making a more sharply angled line.

6 Run in tails

When the knitting is complete, run in the contrasting tails along the backs of stitches in the same color (see page 33).

Project 9: Toy collection

Circular knitting makes great toys for small kids! Choose from kitten and teddy glove puppets, little stuffed mice, or a fun snake. Only small amounts of yarn are required, and the toys don't take long to make.

Finished size: Height approx. 10 in. (25 cm).

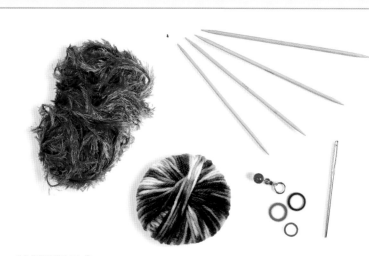

MATERIALS

- Approx. 2 oz (50 gm) double-knitting yarn (approx 120 yds/110 metres to 2 oz/50 gm)
- Scraps of waste yarn
- Set of four double-pointed needles, size US 6 (4 mm), length 8 in. (20 cm)

- Five ring markers, one in color A, four in color B
- Two small buttons for eyes
- One black bead for nose
- 20 in. (50 cm) ribbon, ½ in. (12.5 mm) wide

- 1½-in. (4-cm) square of polyester batting
- Sewing needle and black sewing thread
- Sewing thread to match ribbon
- Tapestry needle to suit yarn

Gauge
Approx. 24 stitches and 30 rounds to 4 in. (10 cm) measured over stockinette stitch, using size US 6 (4 mm) needles. Gauge is not crucial provided a change in size is acceptable, but too loose a gauge may require extra yarn.

Note
You can make this puppet in any double-knitting yarn. Our kitten is made in shade-dyed wool, but you could substitute a fuzzy yarn in a suitable color, or knit the body in stripes (see pages 32–33).

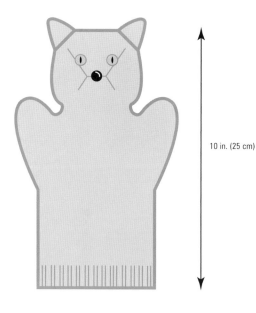

10 in. (25 cm)

Kitten puppet

Our friendly kitten can be quickly knitted on four needles. The arms are shaped like two mitten thumbs, while shaping the head and nose will help you practice various methods of shaping within a round.

MAKING THE BODY

Using two of four size US 6 (4 mm) double-pointed needles and main yarn, cast on 49 sts. Arrange sts on three needles: 16 sts / 16 sts / 17 sts, ending with first cast-on st. Arrange in a triangle with 17 sts on left-hand needle. Slip first cast-on st to right-hand needle and lift last cast-on st over it and off the needle. 48 sts, arranged 16 sts / 16 sts / 16 sts. Place a ring marker before last st of first round. All rounds begin and end 1 st after this marker. Slip it on every round.

Round 1: * K1, P1, * repeat from * to * to end. Repeat this round five more times. 6 rib rounds ending 1 st after marker.

Change to stockinette stitch (all rounds knit) and continue until work measures 3 in. (7.5 cm) in all, ending 1 st after marker.

SHAPE FOR ARMS

Use four ring markers of different colors to mark the positions of the shapings:

Inc round 1: K11, * place marker, m1tbl, K2, m1tbl, place marker, *, K22, repeat from * to *, K11. 52 sts.

Inc rounds 2 & 3: K to end, slipping markers.

Inc round 4: * K to marker, slip marker, m1tbl, K to next marker, m1tbl, slip marker, *, repeat from * to *, K to end. 56 sts.

Repeat last 3 rounds, four more times. 72 sts (14 sts between each pair of markers).

Knit 2 rounds.

Next round: K10, * use tapestry needle to slip next 16 sts onto a holding thread (removing markers), cast on 4 sts using Simple Thumb Cast-on (see page 23), *, K20, repeat from * to *, K10. 48 sts.

Knit 2 rounds.

SHAPE NECK

Next round: K2tog eight times, K16, K2tog eight times. 32 sts.

HEAD

Knit 4 rounds. Make sure sts are arranged 8 sts on 1st needle, 16 sts on 2nd needle and 8 sts on 3rd needle.

1st head round: 1st needle: K to last st, m1tbl, K1. 2nd needle: K1, m1tbl, K to last st, m1tbl, K1. 3rd needle: K1, m1tbl, K to end. 36 sts.

2nd head round: K to end.

Repeat these 2 rounds once more. 40 sts, arranged 10 sts / 20 sts / 10 sts.

SHAPE NOSE

5th head round: 1st needle: K to last st, m1tbl, K1. 2nd needle: K1, m1tbl, K8, m1tbl, place a marker, K2, m1tbl, K8, m1tbl, K1. 3rd needle: K1, m1tbl, K to end. 46 sts. The new marker is the nose marker.

6th head round: K to end, slipping markers.

7th head round: 1st needle: K to last st, m1tbl, K1. 2nd needle: K1, m1tbl, K to nose marker, m1tbl, K2, m1tbl, K to last st, m1tbl, K1. 3rd needle: K1, m1tbl, K to end. 52 sts.

8th head round: K to end, slipping markers.

9th head round: K to nose marker, m1tbl, K2, m1tbl, K to end. 54 sts.

10th head round: K to end, slipping markers.

Repeat 9th and 10th rounds once more, removing nose marker on last round. 56 sts, arranged 12 sts / 32 sts / 12 sts.

13th head round: 1st needle: K. 2nd needle: K13, K2tog, K2, ssk, K13. 3rd needle: K. 54 sts.

14th head round: K to end.

15th head round: 1st needle: K. 2nd needle: K11, K2tog, K4, ssk, K11. 3rd needle: K. 52 sts.

16th head round: K to end.

17th head round: 1st needle: K. 2nd needle: K9, K2tog, K6, ssk, K9. 3rd needle: K. 50 sts.

18th head round: K to end.

19th head round: 1st needle: K. 2nd needle: K7, K2tog, K8, ssk, K7. 3rd needle: K. 48 sts.

20th head round: 1st needle: K. 2nd needle: K5, K2tog, K10, ssk, K5. 3rd needle: K. 46 sts.

21st head round: 1st needle: K. 2nd needle: K3, K2tog, K12, ssk, K3. 3rd needle: K. 44 sts.

Arrange 11 sts / 22 sts / 11 sts.

SHAPE TOP OF HEAD

Dec round 1: 1st needle: K to last 3 sts, K2tog, K1. 2nd needle: K1, ssk, K to last 3 sts, K2tog, K1. 3rd needle: K1, ssk, K to end. 40 sts.

Dec round 2: K to end.

Repeat dec round 1, three more times. 28 sts. K first 7 sts of next round. Slip these sts onto same needle as last 7 sts of round, making 14 sts on each of two needles. Place the needles side by side and bind off the two sets of sts together (see page 41). Cut yarn, leaving a 4-in. (10-cm) tail.

To use your puppet, put your thumb inside one arm and your third and fourth fingers (or just your fourth finger) in the other arm. Put your remaining fingers inside the head, then wriggle them around to change the puppet's expression. Practice waving, winking, and picking things up!

ARMS (MAKE TWO)

Using a set of four size US 6 (4 mm) double-pointed needles, with right side of work facing, pick up and knit 5 sts from loops of 4 cast-on sts above arm opening. K across 16 sts left on holding thread. 21 sts. Arrange 7 sts on each of three needles. Knit 7 rounds.

Shape top of arm

Dec round 1: K1, * K2tog, K2, * repeat from * to * four more times. 16 sts.

Dec round 2: K to end.

Dec round 3: K2tog eight times. 8 sts. Break yarn leaving an 8-in. (20-cm) tail, thread tail into tapestry needle, and slip through these 8 sts. Gather up and secure firmly in same way as top of Hat, page 61.

EARS (MAKE TWO)

With back of head facing, using two size US 6 (4 mm) double-pointed needles, pick up and K 10 sts from corner of head along shaping dart. Work in rows:

Row 1: K1, P to last st, K1.

Row 2: K3, ssk, K2tog, K3.

Row 3: K1, P to last st, K1.

Row 4: K2, ssk, K2tog, K2.

Row 5: K1, P to last st, K1.

Row 6: K1, ssk, K2tog, K1.

Row 7: K1, P to last st, K1.

Row 8: Ssk, K2tog, pass 1st st over 2nd, cut yarn leaving a 4-in. (10-cm) tail, and pull through last st.

ASSEMBLY

Run in all yarn tails. Fold the batting diagonally to form a triangle and place inside head, with lowest point of triangle at nose position. Pin in place. Using sewing needle and black thread, sew on bead for nose, stitching firmly through both the knitting and the batting. Sew on a button for each eye, on the shaping dart, about one-third of the distance between the nose and each ear. Again, take the stitches through to the batting. Tie ribbon around neck in a bow (loosely enough for three fingers to fit inside head). Stitch bow in place using matching sewing thread.

EYES AND NOSES

If you are making a puppet for a child under three years, the use of beads and buttons is not recommended. Embroider the eyes and noses with scraps of yarn of a suitable color, or sew on shapes cut from felt.

All kinds of buttons and beads can be used to make suitable eyes. For the kitten, we used two small, green, two-hole buttons, arranging them with the holes aligned vertically so that the stitches between them (in black) would resemble a cat's eye. For the teddy, we used two small brown buttons, with two smaller black beads sewn on top of the buttons. For both noses, we used black beads approx. ⅜ in. (1 cm) across.

If you prefer, you can purchase toy safety eyes made of plastic, with a push-on back plate. Simply push the stalk of each eye through the knitting, between two stitches, taking care not to fray the knitting yarn. Then push on the back plate firmly to secure the eye.

Teddy bear puppet

Use the same pattern to make a teddy bear puppet: we used 2 oz (50 gm) silky eyelash yarn in a suitable color. The only difference is the shape of the ears, as below:

TEDDY BEAR EARS (MAKE TWO)

Pick up 10 sts as for kitten puppet.

Row 1: K to end.
Row 2: K1, P to last st, K1.
Row 3: K1, * m1tbl, K2, * repeat from * to *three more times, m1tbl, K1. 15 sts.
Row 4: Repeat row 2.
Now work short row shaping as pages 62–64:
Row 5: K9, wrap next st, turn, leaving 6 sts unworked.
Row 6: P3, wrap next st, turn, leaving 6 sts unworked.
Row 7: K5, wrap next st, turn.
Row 8: P7, wrap next st, turn.
Continue in this way working 2 more sts on each row until all 15 sts have been purled on row 12. Bind off.

By using a furry yarn, and adding different ears and eyes, the basic puppet pattern becomes a cuddly teddy bear.

Finished size: Approx. 4½ in. (6.5 cm), excluding tail

MATERIALS

■ Approx. ½ oz
(15 gm) double-
knitting yarn (120
yds/110 metres to
2 oz/50gm) in color A
■ Approx. ½ oz (15
gm) double-knitting
yarn in color B

■ Set of four double-
pointed needles, size
US 5 (3.75 mm),
length 8 in. (20 cm)
■ Two double-pointed
needles, size US 2
(2.75 mm), any length

■ Three black beads
approx. ³⁄₁₆ in.
(4 mm) across
■ Sewing needle and
black sewing thread
■ Polyester toy filling
■ Tapestry needle to
suit yarn
■ Two pins

Gauge
26 stitches and 34 rounds to 4 in.
(10 cm) measured over stockinette
stitch, using size US 5 (3.75 mm)
needles. Note that this is slightly tighter
than the usual recommended gauge for
double-knitting yarn, to make a

firm fabric that will not gape when the
toy is filled.
Gauge is not crucial provided a change
in size is acceptable, but a loose gauge
will give an untidy result and extra yarn
may be required.

See also:
I-cord (page 98)
Picking Up Stitches (pages
54–55)
Abbreviations (page 44)

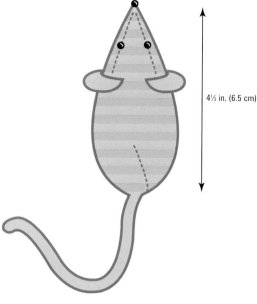

4½ in. (6.5 cm)

Stripy mouse

This little mouse is quick and fun to knit on four
needles. Only small amounts of yarn are needed,
so you can use up all your yarn scraps, making a
collection of mice to give to your friends!

MAKING THE TAIL AND BODY
Begin at tail:
Using two size US 2 (2.75 mm) double-pointed
needles and color A, cast on 4 sts. Knit an I-cord
6 in. (15 cm) long (see page 98).
Change to size US 5 (3.75 mm) needles.
Next row: K1, Ktw, Ktw, K1. 6 sts.
Arrange 2 sts on each of three needles. Arrange
needles in a triangle.
Now work in rounds of stockinette stitch (all
rounds knit):
Preparation round: K1, place ring marker on right-
hand needle, K5. (This marker is 1 st after first st of
round, not 1 st before last st, as is more usual.) All
rounds begin and end 1 st before this marker.
Join in color B. (Do not cut color A, leave it aside.)
Round 1: Using color B, * K1, Ktw, * repeat from *
to * two more times. 9 sts. (3 sts on each needle.)
Round 2: Using B, * K2, Ktw, * repeat from * to *
two more times. 12 sts.
Leave B aside and change to color A, bringing it up
behind B so that the yarns cross. Pull gently on A
to tighten the last st in this color.
Round 3: Using A, * K to last st on needle, Ktw, *
repeat from * to * two more times. 15 sts.
Round 4: Using A, repeat round 3. 18 sts.
Leave A aside and change to color B, bringing it up
behind A so that the yarns cross. Pull gently on B
to tighten the last st in this color.

Round 5: Using B, repeat round 3. 21 sts.
Round 6: Using B, repeat round 3. 24 sts.
Round 7: Using A, repeat round 3. 27 sts.
Round 8: Using A, repeat round 3. 30 sts.
Round 9: Using B, K to end.
Round 10: Using B, repeat round 3. 33 sts.
Round 11: Using A, K to end.
Round 12: Using A, repeat round 3. 36 sts. (12 sts on each needle.)
At this point, it is a good idea to run in the starting tail of color B (see page 33), because it will be difficult to access later.
Now continue in stripes without shaping until body measures 3 in. (7.5 cm) from last row of tail, ending with first round of a stripe in color A.

MARK POSITIONS FOR EARS
Next round: Using A, K14, P8, K4, P8, K14.

SHAPE HEAD
Continue in stripes as set.
Dec round 1: Using B, * K4, ssk, K2tog, K4, * repeat from * to * two more times. 30 sts.
Knit 1 round in B and 2 rounds in A.
Dec round 5: Using B, * K3, ssk, K2tog, K3, * repeat from * to * two more times. 24 sts.
Knit 1 round in B and 2 rounds in A.
Dec round 9: Using B, * K2, ssk, K2tog, K2, * repeat from * to * two more times. 18 sts.
Knit 1 round in B and 2 rounds in A.
Dec round 13: Using B, * K1, ssk, K2tog, K1, * repeat from * to * two more times. 12 sts.
Knit 1 round in B and 2 rounds in A.
Cut B, leaving a 6-in. (15-cm) tail, and run in this tail. Cut A, leaving an 8-in. (20-cm) tail, and thread this tail into a tapestry needle. Slip it through remaining 12 sts, removing the needles. Fill the mouse with toy filling, pushing it down firmly a little at a time to make the body firm and smooth. Gather up the remaining 12 sts left on the thread and secure firmly in the same way as on the top of the Hat on page 61.

EARS (MAKE TWO)
With tail of mouse toward you, using two size US 5 (3.75 mm) double-pointed needles and color A, leave an 8-in. (20-cm) tail of A, then pick up and K 8 sts from loops of one set of P sts made at ear position. Work in rows, not rounds:
Row 1: P to end.
Row 2: K to end.
Repeat these 2 rows once more and row 1 once again. 5 rows, ending P row.
Row 6: Ssk, K4, K2tog. 6 sts.
Row 7: P to end.
Bind off, working first 2 sts as ssk and last 2 sts as

K2tog. Cut yarn, leaving a 6-in. (15-cm) tail. Thread the 8-in. (20-cm) starting tail of A into a tapestry needle. Take a small backstitch through the body at the base of the ear, then run the needle through the stitches all around the edge of the ear and pull up slightly to shape the ear into a curve. Take another small backstitch through the body and run in the tail through the body. Run in the remaining tail down the side of the ear.

ASSEMBLY
Use pins to mark positions for two eyes, on the shaping darts, about halfway between the tip of the nose and the ears. Use sewing needle and black sewing thread to firmly stitch one bead at the tip of the nose. Run the needle through the body to one eye position and stitch on a second bead. Push the needle straight through the head to the second eye position and stitch on the third bead. Take the needle back and forth between the two eye beads, pulling firmly to shape the head, and stitch the beads securely in place. Fasten off with two backstitches underneath a bead, then run in the thread end inside the body.

Plain mouse
For a plain-colored mouse, you will need approx. 1 oz (25 gm) of double-knitting yarn. Knit as for Stripy Mouse, using one color throughout.

TIPS
• You could make a smaller mouse using 4-ply fingering yarn and correspondingly smaller needles. Make the tail about 4 in. (10 cm) long and the body about 2¼ in. (5.5 cm) long from top of tail to ears.
• You could also make a larger mouse in heavier yarn. For the body, choose needles one or two sizes smaller than the needle size recommended on the ball band, and two sizes smaller again for the tail. Adjust the lengths of tail and body to suit the size of your mouse.

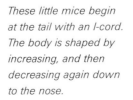

These little mice begin at the tail with an I-cord. The body is shaped by increasing, and then decreasing again down to the nose.

Finished length: Approx. 24 in. (60 cm)

MATERIALS

- Approx. 2 oz (50 gm) aran-weight yarn (98 yds/90 metres to 2 oz/50 gm) in color A
- Approx. 18 yds (20 metres) of aran-weight yarn in color B for spiral pattern
- Scrap of 4-ply fingering yarn in black for tongue
- Scrap of waste yarn

- Set of four double-pointed needles, size US 7 (4.5 mm), length 8 in. (20 cm)
- Two double-pointed needles, size US 1 (2.25 mm), length 6 or 8 in. (15 or 20 cm)
- Bobbin
- Tapestry needle to suit yarn
- Toy filling

- Two black beads
- Sewing needle to fit beads
- Black sewing thread

Gauge

20 stitches and 28 rounds to 4 in. (10 cm) measured over stockinette stitch, using size US 7 (4.5 mm) needles. Note that this is slightly tighter than the usual recommended gauge for aran-weight yarn, to make a firm fabric that will not gape when the toy is filled. Gauge is not crucial provided a change in size is acceptable, but a loose gauge will give an untidy result and extra yarn may be required.

24 in. (60 cm)

Snake

Our slinky snake is made entirely on double-pointed needles, using only small amounts of yarn. We chose green for the main color and added the traveling spiral line in gold lurex, but you can choose any colors you like.

MAKING THE BODY

Wind color B onto the bobbin.

Begin at mouth:

Using two of four size US 7 (4.5 mm) double-pointed needles and waste yarn, cast on 13 sts. Arrange sts on three needles: 4 sts / 5 sts / 4 sts. Knit 1 round.
Change to color A, leaving a 10-in. (25-cm) tail at start.
Knit 4 rounds.

SHAPE HEAD

Inc round: 1st needle: K to last st, m1tbl, K1. 2nd needle: K1, m1tbl, K to last st, m1tbl, K1. 3rd needle: K1, m1tbl, K to end. 17 sts.
Knit 1 round.
Repeat these 2 rounds twice more. 25 sts, 8 rounds in A.

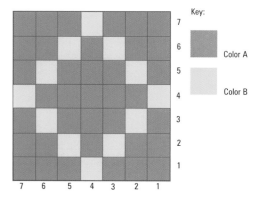

Key:

Color A

Color B

Chart round 1: 1st needle: K7. 2nd needle: K2, K7 sts from 1st row of chart (joining in B on center st and leaving a 12-in. (30-cm) tail of B to the left), K rem 2 sts in A. 3rd needle: K7 in A.
Knit 5 more rounds, reading from chart rows 2–6 in position as set. Use the 12-in. (30-cm) tail of B to knit the B sts left of center, and the main end of B to knit the B sts to right of center.
Knit 1 round, reading from chart row 7 in position as set, using the main end of B to knit the st in B. See page 83 for how to work the traveling line:
Spiral round: In A, K up to st in B, K this st in A, K next st in B, change to A, K to end.
Next round: 1st needle: In A, K to last 3 sts, K2tog, K1. 2nd needle: In A, K1, ssk, K up to st in B, K this

st in A, K next st in B, change to A, K to last 3 sts, K2tog, K1. 3rd needle: In A, K1, ssk, K to end. 21 sts.

Arrange 7 sts on each of three needles.

Now repeat spiral round until snake measures 21 in. (52.5 cm), or length required.

SHAPE TAIL

Dec round: In A, K to st in B, K this st in A, K next st in B, change to A, ssk, K to end.

Re-arranging sts as necessary to work decreasing, repeat this round until 3 sts remain, 1 on each needle. Cut A and B, leaving 6-in. (15-cm) tails. (**Note:** If you are knitting the snake without the traveling line pattern, work decreasing as follows: Place a ring marker, * ssk, K all around ending at marker, slip marker * repeat from * to * until 3 sts remain.)

Thread yarn tail A into a tapestry needle and pass it through remaining 3 sts. Pull up tightly and secure with a backstitch. Run in yarn tail A down a straight line of sts. Run in yarn tail B through the sts of same color.

FORKED TONGUE

Using two size US 1 (2.25 mm) double-pointed needles and color C, cast on 6 sts. Work an I-cord for 1 in. (2.5 cm)—see page 98.

Slip first 3 sts on needle onto a holder and continue working I-cord on rem 3 sts for a further ½ in. (1.5 cm). Bind off and cut yarn, leaving a 4-in. (10-cm) tail.

Return to 3 sts left on holder and K across them. Work I-cord to match first half, bind off, and cut yarn as before.

ASSEMBLY

Turn head inside out to run in starting tail of B along backs of sts in same color. Fill the snake with toy filling, pushing it down evenly with the blunt end of a large knitting needle.

The snake's body is a tapering tube, knitted from the head down to the tail. The black forked tongue is formed from an I-cord.

Thread starting tail of A into tapestry needle and pass it through all loops of first round in A. Remove waste yarn. Place cast-on end of tongue inside mouth, then pull up A tightly to close the mouth. Work two or three firm stitches through tongue to hold it in place, and run in the tail of A. Run in tails at ends of tongue. Run in any remaining tails. Using a sewing needle and black thread, sew on beads for eyes, about halfway along the darts that shape the head.

TIPS

- For color B, we used 3 strands of 4-ply lurex yarn (metallic gold), wound together to make a yarn equivalent in thickness to aran-weight yarn.
- You can make this snake in any yarn you choose. For the body, use needles one size smaller than recommended on ball band and work to a suitable length before shaping the tail. In DK yarn, the snake will be narrower; in bulky yarn, it will be wider.
- You can also make the snake without the spiral pattern, perhaps choosing a random-dyed yarn to add interest.
- Alternatively, try making a striped snake using odds and ends of different colors from your yarn stash (see Knitting Stripes, pages 32–33).

See also:

Traveling Lines (page 83)
Provisional Cast-on (page 52)
I-cord (page 98)
Abbreviations (page 44)

Project 10: Family sweaters

Now that you've learned all the tricks in the book, you're ready to tackle a bigger project with confidence. Choose the basic sweater (maybe in a multi-color or fancy yarn), or add bands of fairisle pattern for the second version, or knit the third version with lacy heart motifs and an open collar.

Finished size: See sizes in chart below

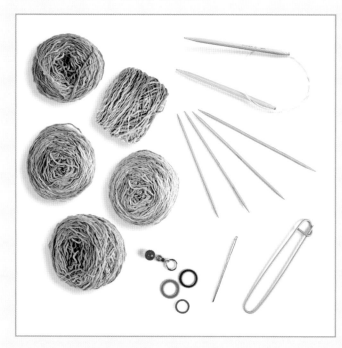

MATERIALS

■ Aran-weight yarn (approx. 100 yds/90 metres to 50 gm):

10	13	15	18	20 oz
(250	350	400	500	550 gm)

For body and yoke
■ Circular needles, sizes US 6 (4 mm) and US 8 (5 mm), approx. length 16 [20, 20, 24, 28] in. (40 [50, 50, 60, 80] cm) (or use double-pointed needles of suitable length)

For sleeves
■ Sets of double-pointed needles sizes US 6 (4 mm) and US 8 (5 mm), approx. length 8 [8, 10, 10, 10] in. (20 [20, 25, 25, 25] cm)

■ Four stitch holders
■ Lengths of waste yarn
■ Tapestry needle to suit yarn
■ Eight ring markers of one color, plus one of another color

Gauge
18 stitches and 24 rounds to 4 in. (10 cm) measured over stockinette stitch, using size US 8 (5 mm) needles. Correct gauge is important to obtain a correct fit. Check the gauge as shown page 42. Alternatively, begin with a sleeve—but be prepared to pull it out and start again if gauge is incorrect.

Note
Instructions for the four larger sizes are given in brackets, like this:
1st size [2nd size, **3rd size,** 4th size, **5th size**].

SIZES

To fit chest	22–24	26–28	30–32	34–36	38–40 in.
	56–61	66–71	76–81	86–91	96–102 cm
Actual measurement	26	30	34	38	42 in.
	66	76	86	96	107 cm
Length to back neck	16½	19¾	21¾	23	26 in.
(adjustable)	42	50	55.5	58.5	66 cm
Sleeve seam	11	14	16	17	19 in.
(adjustable)	28	35.5	40.5	44	48 cm

Diagram 1 Basic sweater layout

Yoke in 8 sections

Sleeve

Sleeve

Body

Basic sweater

Our circular-knit sweater looks great in a multi-color aran-weight yarn, but you can choose any yarn you like that knits to the recommended gauge. Choose the most suitable chest measurement from the sizes given; the lengths of the body and sleeves are adjustable.

MAKING THE BODY

Using a circular needle size US 6 (4 mm), cast on **117** [133, **153**, 169, **189**] sts. Arrange them in a circle without twisting (see page 24). Slip first cast-on st from left-hand needle to right-hand needle and lift last cast-on st over it. **116** [132, **152**, 168, **188**] sts. Place ring marker. All rounds begin and end at this marker.

Round 1: * K2, P2, repeat from * to end of round, slip marker.

Repeat round 1 until work measures **2** [2, **2**, 2½, **2½**] in. (**5** [5, **5**, 6, **6**] cm), ending at marker. Change to size US 8 (5 mm) circular needle. Now work in stockinette (all rounds knit) until work measures **9¼** [11½, **12¼**, 13, **15**] in. (**23.5** [29, **31**, 33, **38**] cm), ending 5 sts before marker. Cut yarn, leaving a 12-in. (30-cm) tail. (Total length may be adjusted here: knit to length required at back neck, less **7¼** [8¼, **9½**, 10, **11**] in. (**18.5** [21, **23**, 25, **27.5**] cm.)

Slip next 10 sts onto first stitch holder. Slip next **48** [**56**, **66**, **74**, **84**] sts onto spare circular needle or a length of yarn for Back. Slip next 10 sts onto second holder. Slip next **48** [56, **66**, 74, **84**] sts onto spare circular needle or another length of yarn for Front.

Set work to one side.

SLEEVES (MAKE TWO)

Using two size US 6 (4 mm) double-pointed needles, cast on **33** [37, **41**, 45, **45**] sts. Arrange sts evenly on three needles, without twisting (see pages 24–25). Slip first cast-on st from left needle to right needle and lift last cast-on st over it. **32** [36, **40**, 44, **44**] sts.

Round 1: * K2, P2, * repeat from * to * to end of round, placing marker before last st. All rounds begin and end 1 st after this marker.

Round 2: * K2, P2, * repeat from * to * to end, slipping marker.

Repeat round 2 until work measures **2** [2, **2**, 2½, **2½**] in. (**5** [5, **5**, 6, **6**] cm), ending 1 st after marker. Change to size US 8 (5 mm) double-pointed needles.

Round 1: K1, m1tbl, K to marker, m1tbl, slip marker, K1. **34** [38, **42**, 46, **46**] sts.

Knit **8** [**7**, 7, 6, **6**] rounds.
Repeat the last **9** [8, **8**, 7, **7**] rounds until there are **44** [52, **58**, 66, **72**] sts.
Continue in stockinette stitch (all rounds knit) until sleeve measures **11** [14, **16**, 17, **19**] in. (**28** [35.5, **40.5**, 44, **48**] cm), or sleeve length required, ending 4 sts before marker. Cut yarn, leaving a 20-in. (50-cm) tail.
Slip next 10 sts onto a stitch holder, slip next **34** [42, **48**, 56, **62**] sts onto a spare circular needle (or length of yarn).

YOKE

With right side of all pieces facing, begin at right of sts held on circular needle or length of yarn for Back. Slip first **24** [28, **33**, 37, **42**] sts onto another spare needle. This is center back. Using circular needle size US 8 (5 mm), K**23** [27, **32**, 36, **41**] from rem sts left for Back, K last st tog with first st of one sleeve. K across next **32** [40, **46**, 54, **60**] sts of sleeve, K last st tog with first st left for Front. K across next **46** [54, **64**, 72, **82**] sts of Front, K last st tog with first st of remaining sleeve. K across next **32** [40, **46**, 54, **60**] sts of second sleeve, K last st tog with first st of round. **160** [192, **224**, 256, **288**] sts.

Place ring marker. All yoke rounds begin and end at this marker.
The yoke is knitted in eight darted sections, separated by dart markers placed on next round. Choose a different color for the new markers:

See also:
Using Markers (page 31)
Using Stitch Holders (page 53)
Short Row Shaping (pages 62–64)
Bind-off Together (page 41)
Abbreviations (page 44)

Add interest to the basic sweater pattern by choosing a random-dyed yarn.

Preparation round: K10 [12, **14**, 16, **18**] sts, place dart marker, * K20 [24, **28**, 32, **36**], place dart marker, *, repeat from * to * six more times, K remaining 10 [12, **14**, 16, **18**], sts ending at round marker. 8 groups of 20 [24, **28**, 32, **36**] sts. Knit 4 rounds ending at round marker. **

Dec round: Slip round marker, * K to 2 sts before next marker, ssk, slip dart marker, K2tog * repeat from * to * seven more times, K to round marker. 8 groups of 18 [22, **26**, 30, **34**] sts, 6 rounds in all. Knit 5 rounds. 11 rounds in all.
Repeat last 6 rounds, **3** [3, **3**, 2, **2**] more times. 8 groups of **12** [16, **20**, 26, **30**] sts; **29** [29, **29**, 23, **23**] yoke rounds.

***Note:** As the number of stitches decreases, you will need to change to a shorter circular needle, or a set of size US 8 (5 mm) double-pointed needles. On double-pointed needles, the round marker should be replaced before the last st of the round.

Work dec round again. 8 groups of **10** [14, **18**, 24, **28**] sts.
Knit 3 rounds. **33** [33, **33**, 27, **27**] yoke rounds.
Repeat last 4 rounds, **0** [1, **2**, 5, **6**] more times.
8 groups of **10** [12, **14**, 14, **16**] sts; **33** [37, **41**, 47, **51**] yoke rounds.
Work dec round again. 8 groups of **8** [10, **12**, 12, **14**] sts.
Knit 1 round. **35** [39, **43**, 49, **53**] yoke rounds.
Repeat last 2 rounds **0** [1, **1**, 1, **2**] more times.
8 groups of **8** [8, **10**, 10, **10**] sts; **35** [41, **45**, 51, **57**] yoke rounds.

3rd & 4th sizes only
Next round: Slip round marker, * K to next marker, slip marker, K2tog * repeat from * to * to end.

All sizes
64 [64, **72**, 72, **80**] sts; 8 groups of **8** [8, **9**, 9, **10**] sts; **35** [41, **46**, 52, **57**] yoke rounds.

SHAPE COLLAR STAND
The collar stand is worked in short rows, using the wrapped stitch technique (see pages 62–64). Remove the dart markers as you come to them, but leave the round marker in place.
Row 1: K20 [20, **21**, 21, **22**], wrap next st, turn.
Row 2: P40 [40, **42**, 42, **44**], wrap next st, turn.
Row 3: K37 [37, **39**, 39, **41**], wrap next st, turn.
Row 4: P34 [34, **36**, 36, **38**], wrap next st, turn.
Row 5: K31 [31, **33**, 33, **35**], wrap next st, turn.
Row 6: P28 [28, **30**, 30, **32**], wrap next st, turn.
Row 7: K25 [25, **27**, 27, **29**], wrap next st, turn.
Row 8: P22 [22, **24**, 24, **26**], wrap next st, turn.
24 [24, **30**, 30, **36**] sts remain unworked at center front.
Row 9: K11 [11, **12**, 12, **13**] sts ending at center back.

NECKBAND
Change to size US 6 (4 mm) double-pointed needles and work in rounds:
Next round: * K2, P2, repeat from * to * to end, removing any remaining dart markers.
Repeat this round, slipping round marker, until neckband measures 2½ [2½, **3**, 3, **3½**] in. (**6** [6, **7.5**, 7.5, **9**] cm), ending at center back.
Change to size US 8 (5 mm) double-pointed needles and bind off in K and P as set.

ASSEMBLY
At each underarm, bind off together the two sets of stitches left on holders (see page 41), using the 20-in. (50-cm) tails left for this purpose. Run in any remaining yarn ends (see page 33). Block (see page 45).

Fairisle yoke sweater

You might prefer to knit this version of the basic sweater, adding three bands of simple fairisle patterning to the yoke area. A plain wool or wool-blend yarn is recommended, to help the fairisle stitches sit neatly together. Choose any three colors you like.

In addition to the materials given for the Basic Sweater, you will need 1 oz (25 gm) each of two contrast colors, B (green) and C (lilac).

BODY AND SLEEVES

Work as for Basic Sweater.

YOKE WITH FAIRISLE BANDS

Work as given for Basic Sweater Yoke to **.

Round 6 (dec round): Slip round marker, * K to 2 sts before next marker, ssk, slip dart marker, K2tog * repeat from * to * seven more times, K to round marker. 8 groups of **18** [22, **26**, 30, **34**] sts. 6 rounds in all.

Cut color A, leaving a 6-in. (15-cm) tail.

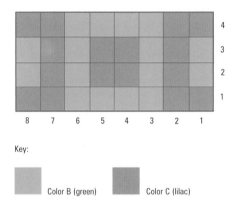

Key:

Color B (green)   Color C (lilac)

Three bands of simple fair-isle patterning are added to the yoke of this version of the basic sweater.

Work fairisle pattern by two-color stranding method (see page 82). B = first contrast (green), C = second contrast (lilac).

Round 7: Read chart row 1 from right to left, repeating the 8 chart sts all around.

Rounds 8–10: Read in same way from chart rows 2–4.

Cut colors B and C, leaving 6-in. (15-cm) tails. Join in color A.

Round 11: K to end.

Repeat rounds 6–11 twice more, ending with round 11. 8 groups of **14** [18, **22**, 26, **30**] sts. 23 yoke rounds in all.

Continue in color A throughout:

1st, 2nd & 3rd sizes only:

Repeat dec round (round 6), K 5 rounds.

All sizes:

8 groups of **12** [16, **20**, 26, **30**] sts; **29** [29, **29**, 23, **23**] rounds.

Complete as Basic Sweater from *** to end.

ASSEMBLY

As for Basic Sweater.

See also:

Stranding (page 82)

Abbreviations (page 44)

Lacy heart sweater

The third version of the sweater features lacy heart motifs on the yoke, and an open collar knitted in rows. Choose a smooth cotton or cotton-blend yarn to show off the stitch details. You will need the same amount of yarn as for the Basic Sweater.

BODY AND SLEEVES

Work as for Basic Sweater, substituting Lacy Rib (see page 116) for the 2 x 2 ribbing.

YOKE

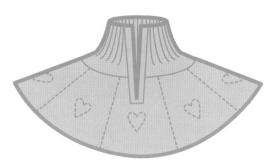

Work as for Basic Sweater yoke to **. 8 groups of **20** [24, **28**, 32, **36**] sts. 5 rounds in all.

3rd, 4th, & 5th sizes only:
Work dec round as for Basic Sweater. K 5 rounds.

All sizes:
8 groups of **20** [24, **26**, 30, **34**] sts; **5** [5, **11**, 11, **11**] rounds in all.
Work dec round once more. K 2 rounds. 8 groups of **18** [22, **24**, 28, **32**] sts; **8** [8, **14**, 14, **14**] rounds in all.

Next round: Remove round marker, K to next dart marker, * slip dart marker, K**8** [10, **11**, 13, **15**], K2tog, K to next dart marker, repeat from * six more times, slip last dart marker, K**8** [10, **11**, 13, **15**], K2tog. 8 groups of **17** [21, **23**, 27, **31**] sts.

HEART MOTIFS

To make the pattern simpler to follow, the heart-motif rounds begin and end at the next dart. Knit to the next dart marker. Remove this dart marker and replace it with the round marker.

Heart round 1: * Slip marker, K**7** [9, **10**, 12, **14**], K2tog, yo, K**8** [10, **11**, 13, **15**], repeat from * to * seven more times, ending at round marker.

Heart round 2: K to end, slipping markers.

Heart round 3: * Slip marker, K**6** [8, **9**, 11, **13**], K2tog, yo, K1, yo, ssk, K**6** [8, **9**, 11, **13**], ssk, repeat from * to * seven more times.

Heart round 4: K to end, slipping markers.

Heart round 5: * Slip marker, K2tog, K**3** [5, **6**, 8, **10**], K2tog, yo, K3, yo, ssk, K**3** [5, **6**, 8, **10**], ssk, *

repeat from * to * seven more times. 8 groups of **15** [19, **21**, 25, **29**] sts.

Heart round 6: K to end, slipping markers.

Heart round 7: * Slip marker, K **3** [5, **6**, 8, **10**], K2tog, yo, K5, yo, ssk, K**3** [5, **6**, 8, **10**], * repeat from * to * seven more times.

Heart round 8: K to end, slipping markers.

Heart round 9: * Slip marker, K**2** [4, **5**, 7, **9**], K2tog, yo, K2, K2tog, yo, K3, yo, ssk, K**2** [4, **5**, 7, **9**], * repeat from * to * seven more times.

Heart round 10: K to end, slipping markers.

Heart round 11: * Slip marker, K2tog, K**2** [4, **5**, 7, **9**], yo, s2togk, yo, K1, yo, s2togk, yo, K**2** [4, **5**, 7, **9**], ssk, * repeat from * to * seven more times. 8 groups of **13** [17, **19**, 23, **27**] sts.

Next round: * Slip marker, K**5** [7, **8**, 10, **12**], K2tog, K**6** [8, **9**, 11, **13**], *, repeat from * to * seven more times. 8 groups of **12** [16, **18**, 22, **26**] sts; **21** [21, **27**, 27, **27**] yoke rounds in all.

1st & 2nd sizes only:
Knit 2 rounds. Work dec round as for Basic Sweater. Work 3 more rounds.

All sizes:
8 groups of **10** [14, **18**, 22, **26**] sts; 27 yoke rounds in all.
Cut yarn, leaving a 6-in. (15-cm) tail. Remove round marker and replace it with a dart marker.
Slip **35** [49, **63**, 77, **91**] sts to center front, midway between two dart markers.

DIVIDE FOR NECK

From this point onward, the yoke is worked in rows, turning at center front to make neck opening.

Special note: A selvage is formed on the edge sts as follows: At end of every row, K last 2 sts. At beginning of 2nd and every following row, bring yarn to front as if to purl (yf), slip the first st purlwise (Sl1p), take yarn through to back to K next st.

Row 1: K all around, ending at center front. Turn work so purl side is facing you.

Row 2 (wrong side): Yf, Sl1p, yb, K1, P to last 2 sts, K2. Turn work.

Row 3: Yf, Sl1p, yb, K to end. Turn work.

Row 4: Repeat row 2. 31 yoke rows in all.

Dec row: Yf, Sl1p, yb, * K to 2 sts before next marker, ssk, slip marker, K2tog, * repeat from * to * seven more times, K to end. **64** [96, **128**, 160, **192**] sts.

Work 3 rows without shaping, ending wrong-side row. 35 yoke rows in all.

Repeat last 4 rows **0** [2, **2**, 3, **4**] more times. 64 [64, **96**, 112, **128**] sts remain; **35** [43, **43**, 47, **51**] yoke rows/rounds in all.

3rd, 4th & 5th sizes only:
Work dec row.

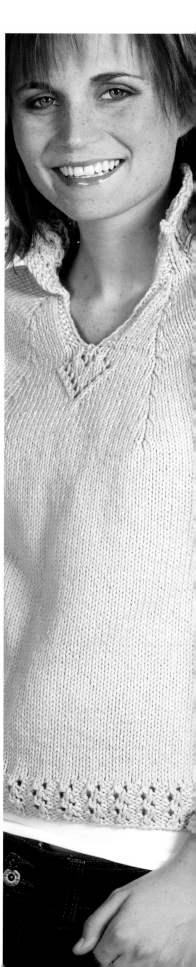

Work 1 wrong-side row.

Repeat last 2 rows **0** [1, **2**] more times.

All sizes:

64 [64, **80**, 80, **80**] sts; 35 [43, **45**, 51, **57**] yoke rows in all.

3rd & 4th sizes only:

Next round: Sl1p, * K to dart marker, K2tog, *, repeat from * to * seven more times, K to end.

Work 1 wrong-side row.

All sizes:

64 [64, **72**, 72, **80**] sts; 35 [43, **47**, 53, **57**] yoke rows in all.

SHAPE COLLAR STAND

See Short Row Shaping (pages 62–64).

Row 1: Sl1p, K to last **9** [12, **15**, 15, **18**] sts, wrap next st, turn.

Row 2: P to last **9** [12, **15**, 15, **18**] sts, wrap next st, turn.

Row 3: K to last **12** [15, **18**, 18, **21**] sts, wrap next st, turn.

Row 4: P to last **12** [15, **18**, 18, **21**] sts, turn.

Work 4 more rows in the same way, leaving 3 more sts unworked at the end of each row, until **18** [21, **24**, 24, **27**] sts are left unworked at each end of 8th (P) row.

Row 9: K to end, working wrapped sts as on page 64.

Row 10: Sl1p, K2, P to last 3 sts, working wrapped sts as on page 64, K3.

COLLAR

Row 1: Sl1p, K2, * P2, K2, * repeat from * to * to last 5 sts, P2, K3.

Row 2: Sl1p, K2, * yo, ssk, P2, * repeat from * to * to last 5 sts, yo, ssk, K3.

Row 3: Repeat row 1.

Row 4: Sl1p, K2, * K2tog, yo, P2, * repeat from * to * to last 5 sts, K2tog, yo, K3.

Repeat these 4 rows until collar measures **2½** [2½, **3**, 3, **3½**] in. (**6.5** [6.5, **7.5**, 7.5, **9**] cm), ending row 2 or 4.

Bind off in rib as set.

ASSEMBLY

As for Basic Sweater. At center front, use yarn tail to backstitch across 2 sts of last round at base of opening, then run in tail on wrong side.

This version of the sweater features Lacy Heart motifs on the yoke, and an open collar. The ribbing and collar are worked in Lacy Rib to add extra texture.

> **See also:**
> Short Row Shaping
> (page 64)
> Abbreviations (page 44)

Finishing touches

These simple techniques require only small amounts of yarn, but they can be used to add the final flourish that completes your project.

An I-cord is the smallest tube you can knit, used for the drawstring for a purse, as on pages 50–51, or the mouse's tail on pages 88–89.

Fringes, tassels, and pompons can be used to decorate many of the projects in this book. Add a fringe to the lower seam of the drawstring bag on pages 50–51, a tassel or pompon to a hat (pages 68–69), or tassels to the pillows on pages 74–77.

I-cord

This cord is a tiny knitted tube. You will need two double-pointed needles, two or three sizes smaller than the size recommended for your yarn.

1 Cast on
Cast on three, four, or five stitches (no more), by any method (see pages 20–23). Knit 1 row in the usual way.

3 Repeat as required
Repeat Step 2 to the length required. The knitting forms a small tube. Pull gently on the finished cord to close the gap where the yarn passes across the back. Bind off.

2 Knit without turning the work
Without turning the work around, hold the needle with the stitches in your left hand. Push the stitches along toward the right needle tip. Bring the yarn across the back of the stitches and pull it tightly to bunch the stitches together, then use the empty needle to knit another row from right to left in the usual way.

This I-cord is used as a drawstring for the drawstring purse on pages 50–51.

See Also
• Drawstring Purse **p51**
• Mice **p88–89**

Fringe

You will need a piece of card, a pair of scissors, and a crochet hook.

1 Wind yarn around card

Decide on the depth of fringe you need. Cut a piece of firm card about ½ in. (1.25 cm) wider than this measurement and 3–4 in. (7–10 cm) wide. For each separate tail of a fringe, you usually need at least two strands of yarn. Wind the yarn around the card to make the number of strands you need.

2 Cut through the strands

Cut through all the strands along one edge of the card. All the strands are more than twice as long as the depth of the fringe you are making.

3 Insert hook to catch loop

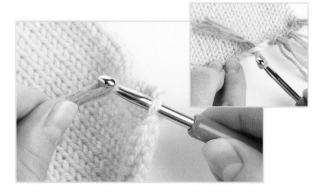

With the right side of the knitting facing you, insert the crochet hook from wrong side to right side along the edge where you want the fringe to be, inserting through a gap between stitches to avoid splitting the yarn. Fold two (or more) strands of yarn in half and catch the loop with the hook. Gently pull the loop through the knitting.

4 Pull tails through loop

Catch all the tails of the strands with the hook, and pull them through the loop. Pull on the tails to tighten the knot.

5 Repeat and trim

Repeat as required. Lay the work flat and trim all the tails to the same length.

A fringe has been used to adapt the drawstring purse on pages 50–51.

Tassel

You will need a piece of firm card, scissors, and a tapestry needle.

1 Wind yarn around card

Decide how long you want the tassel to be—perhaps about 2–4 in. (5–10 cm). Cut a piece of card about ½ in. (1.25 cm) wider than this measurement. Wind the yarn around the card twenty or thirty times, or more, to make a nice plump tassel.

2 Thread tail into needle

Cut the yarn leaving a tail of about 10 in. (25 cm). Thread this tail into the tapestry needle.

3 Bind tail around tassel

Slip the yarn off the card and bind the tail tightly around it, five or six times, about ½ in. (1.25 cm) from one end.

4 Bring needle out at top

Slip the needle underneath the binding and bring it out at the top of the tassel.

5 Catch tops of loops together

Pass the needle through all the small loops at the top of the tassel, catching them all together.

7 Cut and trim tassel

Cut through all the strands at the bottom of the tassel. If they are not quite even, lay the tassel flat and trim them in a straight line. Then use the yarn tail to sew the tassel in place.

6 Knot tail tightly

Knot the tail tightly at the top of the loop. Do not cut it off.

A tassel has been added to the hat on pages 68–69.

See Also

• Hat **p68–69**
• Bolster Pillow **p76–77**

Pompon

Plastic pompon makers can be purchased in various sizes; follow the instructions supplied with the product. Alternatively, you can use cardboard and scissors to make a pompon of any size you want. You will also need a pair of drawing compasses and a tapestry needle.

1 Cut two card circles

Use the compasses to draw two circles on the card, the size you want your pompon to be—about 2–4 in. (5–10 cm) across, perhaps. Draw a smaller circle, about half the size, at the center of each. Cut out the circles and the central holes, making two matching donut shapes.

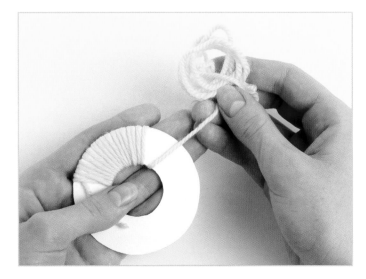

2 Wind yarn around card circles

Place the two circles together and wind lengths of yarn round and round, passing through the center hole, to cover all the cardboard evenly. You can use several colors if you wish.

3 Wind until hole is full

When the hole at the center gets too small for your fingers, thread the yarn into a tapestry needle and carry on winding until the hole is full.

4 Cut through the strands

Part the strands on the edge of the circles and insert the tip of the scissors between the two layers of card. Cut through all the strands around the edge of the circles. If the central hole is full, the strands will not slip out of place.

6 Remove card circles

Carefully cut through both card circles from the outside edge to the center, and pull them away gently. Fluff up the pompon and snip off any untidy ends. Then use the long tail from Step 5 to sew the pompon in place.

5 Tie around center

Pull the card circles slightly apart and tie a strand of yarn tightly around the center. Leave one tail of about 8 in. (20 cm) to use for sewing on the pompon; cut the other tail to match the pompon strands.

Pompons have been added to the drawstring purse design on pages 50–51.

See Also

• Drawstring Purse (variation) **p51**

chapter three
Stitch Library

The stitch patterns in this library are arranged in order of complexity, beginning with basic stitches such as stockinette and rib patterns, followed by other simple combinations of knit and purl stitches, producing textured patterns. More complex textures are then shown, using cables, twist stitches, slip stitches, lace stitches, bobbles, leaves, and little tails. A selection of fairisle patterns in two-color knitting is included, and finally, some interesting multi-color patterns using the technique of traveling lines.

All these stitch patterns are written specifically for circular knitting, and are suitable for working on either a circular needle or on a set of double-pointed needles.

1 Stockinette Stitch

This is the most basic stitch of all. Worked in circular knitting, all rounds are knitted, so it's even easier than the two-needle version.

May be worked on any number of sts.

Round 1: K to end.

Repeat this round.

2 Reverse Stockinette Stitch

If you want the reverse (purl) side of stockinette stitch to be on the right side of your work, simply purl every round.

May be worked on any number of sts.

Round 1: P to end.

Repeat this round.

3 1 x 1 Rib

This stitch is often used at the beginning or at the end of a piece of knitting, to prevent the edge from rolling over.

Requires an even number of sts.

Round 1: * K1, P1, * repeat * to * to end.

Repeat this round.

TIP

You can knit rib patterns with any combination of knit and purl stitches, such as K3, P3, or K5, P2, or K1, P7. The total number of stitches must be a multiple of the number of stitches in each repeat. For example:

K3, P3 rib requires a multiple of 6 sts.

K5, P2 rib requires a multiple of 7 sts.

K1, P7 rib requires a multiple of 8 sts.

4 2 x 2 Rib

Firmer and more elastic than 1 x 1 rib, this stitch also prevents edges from curling.
Requires a multiple of 4 sts.

Round 1: * K2, P2, * repeat * to * to end.
Repeat this round.

5 Seed Stitch

This stitch also produces flat edges, but it does not have the elasticity of a rib stitch.
Requires an even number of sts.

Round 1: * K1, P1, * repeat from * to * to end.
Round 2: * P1, K1, * repeat from * to * to end.
Repeat these 2 rounds.
Note that on the 2nd and every following round, you purl the knit stitches and knit the purl stitches of the previous round.

6 Double Seed Stitch

This stitch has similar properties to seed stitch (above), but with a bolder texture.
Requires an even number of sts.

Round 1: * K1, P1, * repeat from * to * to end.
Round 2: Repeat round 1.
Round 3: * P1, K1, * repeat from * to * to end.
Round 4: Repeat round 3.
Repeat these 4 rounds.

1 Garter Stitch

In row-by-row knitting, garter stitch is produced by knitting every row. In circular knitting, alternate knit and purl rounds are required to produce the same stitch. May be worked on any number of sts.

Round 1: K to end.
Round 2: P to end.
Repeat these 2 rounds.

2 Ridge Stitch

Wider ridges are formed by working several purl rounds, with any number of knit rounds between the ridges. The ridges shown here are three rounds wide, but you can change the width as you wish.
May be worked on any number of sts.

Rounds 1–3: K to end.
Rounds 4–6: P to end.
Repeat these 6 rounds.

3 Caterpillar Stitch

In this stitch, groups of purl stitches stand out against a stockinette-stitch background.
Requires a multiple of 6 sts.

Rounds 1 & 2: K to end.
Round 3: * K1, P4, K1, * repeat from * to * to end.
Rounds 4 & 5: K to end.
Round 6: * P2, K2, P2, * repeat from * to * to end.
Repeat these 6 rounds.

4 Knotted Check Stitch

Here, purl stitches are arranged to form little "knots" on a stockinette-stitch background.

Requires a multiple of 6 sts.

Round 1: * P1, K1, P1, K3, * repeat from * to * to end.

Round 2: * P3, K3, * repeat from * to * to end.

Round 3: Repeat round 1.

Round 4: K to end.

Round 5: * K3, P1, K1, P1, * repeat from * to * to end.

Round 6: * K3, P3, * repeat from * to * to end.

Round 7: Repeat round 5.

Round 8: K to end.

Repeat these 8 rounds.

5 Small Checkerboard

This pattern alternates blocks of stockinette stitch in a checkerboard pattern with blocks of reverse stockinette stitch.

Requires a multiple of 6 sts.

Rounds 1–4: * K3, P3, * repeat from * to * to end.

Rounds 5–8: * P3, K3, * repeat from * to * to end.

Repeat these 8 rounds.

6 Seed Stitch Checkerboard

This pattern alternates blocks of seed stitch with blocks of stockinette stitch, for a differently textured effect.

Requires a multiple of 10 sts.

Round 1: * [P1, K1] twice, P1, K5, * repeat from * to * to end.

Round 2: * [K1, P1] twice, K6, * repeat from * to * to end.

Rounds 3–5: Repeat rounds 1 and 2 once more and round 1 once again.

Round 6: * K5, [P1, K1] twice, P1, * repeat from * to * to end.

Round 7: * K6, [P1, K1] twice, * repeat from * to * to end.

Rounds 8–10: Repeat rounds 6 and 7 once more and round 6 once again.

Repeat these 10 rounds.

1 Garter Blocks

Tiny blocks of garter stitch alternate with blocks of stockinette stitch for an interesting effect. Requires a multiple of 8 sts.

Round 1: * P4, K4, * repeat from * to * to end.
Round 2: K to end.
Rounds 3 & 4: Repeat rounds 1 and 2.
Round 5: * K4, P4, * repeat from * to * to end.
Round 6: K to end.
Rounds 7 & 8: Repeat rounds 5 and 6.
Repeat these 8 rounds.

2 Broken ridges

Ridges of reverse stockinette stitch are broken by pairs of stockinette stitches, making a bold texture. Requires a multiple of 8 sts.

Rounds 1–3: * K1, P6, K1, * repeat from * to * to end.
Round 4: K to end.
Rounds 5–7: * P3, K2, P3, * repeat from * to * to end.
Round 8: K to end.
Repeat these 8 rounds.

3 Basketweave

This basketweave pattern is made by alternating blocks of garter stitch with blocks of 1 x 1 rib. Requires a multiple of 10 sts.

Round 1: * [K1, P1] twice, K6, * repeat from * to * to end.
Round 2: * [K1, P1] twice, K1, P5, * repeat from * to * to end.
Rounds 3–5: Repeat rounds 1 and 2 once more, and round 1 once again.
Round 6: * K6, [P1, K1] twice, * repeat from * to * to end.
Round 7: * P5, K1, [P1, K1] twice, * repeat from * to * to end.
Rounds 8–10: Repeat rounds 6 and 7 once more, and round 6 once again.
Repeat these 10 rounds.

4 Diagonal Rib

Ribs of knit and purl stitches move diagonally across the work, spiraling around a tube of circular knitting.
Requires a multiple of 4 sts.

Round 1: * K2, P2, * repeat from * to * to end.
Round 2: * K1, P2, K1, * repeat from * to * to end.
Round 3: * P2, K2, * repeat from * to * to end.
Round 4: * P1, K2, P1, * repeat from * to * to end.
Repeat these 4 rounds.

5 Zigzag Rib

By changing the direction of diagonal ribs, a zigzag pattern is formed.
Requires a multiple of 6 sts.

Round 1: * K3, P3, * repeat from * to * to end.
Round 2: * K2, P3, K1, * repeat from * to * to end.
Round 3: * K1, P3, K2, * repeat from * to * to end.
Round 4: * P3, K3, * repeat from * to * to end.
Round 5: Repeat round 3.
Round 6: Repeat round 2.
Repeat these 6 rounds.

6 Seed Stitch Diamonds

Seed stitches can be arranged in many ways to form textured patterns like these tiny diamonds.
Requires a multiple of 6 sts.

Round 1: * P1, K5, * repeat from * to * to end.
Round 2: * K1, P1, K3, P1, * repeat from * to * to end.
Round 3: * P1, K1, * repeat from * to * to end.
Round 4: Repeat round 2.
Round 5: Repeat round 1.
Round 6: * K3, P1, K2, * repeat from * to * to end.
Round 7: * K2, P1, K1, P1, K1, * repeat from * to * to end.
Round 8: * K1, P1, * repeat from * to * to end.
Round 9: Repeat round 7.
Round 10: Repeat round 6.
Repeat these 10 rounds.

1 Small Cable Rib

Small four-stitch cables alternate with purl stitches to form a firm, elastic rib, a suitable substitute for plain ribbing on a garment.

Requires a multiple of 8 sts.

Round 1: * P2, K4, P2, * repeat from * to * to end.
Round 2: * P2, C4R, P2, * repeat from * to * to end.
Rounds 3 & 4: Repeat round 1.

Repeat these 4 rounds.

2 Cable and Garter Stitch

This wider cable on a garter-stitch background makes a fabric suitable for the body of a garment. The number of garter stitches between cables may be increased as desired.

Requires a multiple of 10 sts.

Round 1: * P2, K6, P2, * repeat from * to * to end.
Round 2: K to end.
Round 3: * P2, C6R, P2, * repeat from * to * to end.
Round 4: Repeat round 2.
Rounds 5–8: Repeat rounds 1 and 2, twice.

3 Honeycomb Stitch

This all-over cable pattern makes a firm, crunchy texture. It is often worked as a panel with plainer stitches at either side.

Requires a multiple of 8 sts.

Round 1: K to end.
Round 2: * C4R, C4L, * repeat from * to * to end.
Rounds 3 & 4: K to end.
Round 5: * C4L, C4R, * repeat from * to * to end.
Round 6: K to end.

Repeat these 6 rounds.

4 Double Cable Panel

Wide cables like this one may be worked into a plain garment to add strong vertical interest. To make the cable longer, work more rounds between the cable rounds. Panel requires 12 sts.

Round 1: K to required position for panel, P2, K8, P2, K to end.

Rounds 2 & 3: Repeat round 1.

Round 4 (cable round): K to panel, P2, C4R, C4L, P2, K to end.

Rounds 5 & 6: Repeat round 1.

Repeat these 6 rounds.

5 Large Braid Panel

Here, the arrangement of cables produces a braided effect. Panel requires 11 sts.

Round 1: K to required position for panel, P1, K9, P1, K to end.

Round 2: Repeat round 1.

Round 3: K to panel, P1, K3, C6L, P1, K to end.

Rounds 4–6: Repeat round 1.

Round 7: K to panel, P1, C6R, K3, P1, K to end.

Round 8: Repeat round 1.

Repeat these 8 rounds.

6 Cable Blocks

Simple cables are arranged in a checkerboard pattern with blocks of reverse stockinette stitch.

Requires a multiple of 12 sts.

Rounds 1–4: * K6, P6, * repeat from * to * to end.

Round 5: * C6R, P6, * repeat from * to * to end.

Rounds 6–8: Repeat round 1.

Rounds 9–12: * P6, K6, * repeat from * to * to end.

Round 13: * P6, C6R, * repeat from * to * to end.

Rounds 14–16: Repeat round 9.

Repeat these 16 rounds.

TIPS

- For technique of working cables, see page 72.
- When working on double-pointed needles, arrange the stitches in such a way that the stitches forming any cable group are all on the same needle.
- When working cable panels, use a ring marker, see page 31, at either side of the panel stitches to help you position the panel correctly.

1 Twisted Rib

This stitch makes a firm, ribbed pattern suitable for edging garments.

Requires a multiple of 4 sts.

Round 1: * P2, Tw2L, * repeat from * to * to end.

Repeat this round.

2 Mock Cable Rib

Twisted stitches may be arranged to imitate true cables, although the appearance is slightly flatter.

Requires a multiple of 6 sts.

Round 1: * P3, Tw2L, K1, * repeat from * to * to end.

Round 2: * P3, K3, * repeat from * to * to end.

Round 3: * P3, K1, Tw2L, * repeat from * to * to end.

Round 4: Repeat round 2.

Repeat these 4 rounds.

3 Herringbone Stitch

Twisted stitches arranged on a stockinette-stitch background make a firm, stable knitted fabric.

Requires a multiple of 4 sts.

Round 1: * Tw2L, K2, * repeat from * to * to end.

Round 2: * K1, Sl1p, K2, * repeat from * to * to end.

Round 3: * K1, Tw2L, K1, * repeat from * to * to end.

Round 4: * K2, Sl1p, K1, * repeat from * to * to end.

Round 5: * K2, Tw2L, * repeat from * to * to end.

Round 6: * K3, Sl1p, * repeat from * to * to end.

Round 7: * K2, Tw2R, * repeat from * to * to end.

Round 8: Repeat round 4.

Round 9: * K1, Tw2R, K1, * repeat from * to * to end.

Round 10: Repeat round 2.

Round 11: * Tw2R, K2, * repeat from * to * to end.

Round 12: * Sl1p, K3, * repeat from * to * to end.

Repeat these 12 rounds.

Special Abbreviations

Tw2L = twist 2 sts to left (page 70)

Tw2R = twist 2 sts to right (page 71)

4 Brick Pattern

This all-over textured stitch is made by winding the yarn twice to make a longer stitch, then slipping this stitch on subsequent rounds, in a simple brick arrangement.

Requires a multiple of 6 sts.

Round 1: * P5, K1wtw, * repeat from * to * to end.
Round 2: * K5, Sl1del, * repeat from * to * to end.
Rounds 3 & 4: * K5, Sl1p, * repeat from * to * to end.
Round 5: * P2, K1wtw, P3, * repeat from * to * to end.
Round 6: * K2, Sl1del, K3, * repeat from * to * to end.
Rounds 7 & 8: * K2, Sl1p, K3, * repeat from * to * to end.

Repeat these 8 rounds.

5 Two-color Check

By working the rounds in alternating colors, this slip-stitch pattern makes a simple all-over check. Carry the color not in use up the wrong side of the work, and always bring the new color up behind the old color when changing colors, so that the yarns cross on the wrong side.

Requires a multiple of 4 sts.

Round 1: Using color A, * K3, K1 winding yarn 3 times around ndl, * repeat from * to * to end.
Round 2: Using color B, * K3, Sl1del, * repeat from * to * to end.
Round 3: Using color B, * K3, Sl1p, * repeat from * to * to end.

Repeat these 3 rounds.

6 Vertical Stripes

This two-color slip-stitch pattern makes a firm, ridged fabric. It is very simple to work.

Requires a multiple of 4 sts.

Round 1 (preparation round): Using color A, * K1, K1wtw, K2, * repeat from * to * to end.
Round 2: Using color B, * K1, sl1del, K1, K1wtw, * repeat from * to * to end.
Round 3: Using color A, * K1, K1wtw, K1, sl1del, * repeat from * to * to end.

Repeat rounds 2 and 3.

Special Abbreviations

K1wtw = K1, winding yarn twice around needle.

Sl1del = slip 1 purlwise dropping extra loop(s)

1 Lacy Rib

Substitute this rib for a standard 2 x 2 rib (page 107) for a lighter, more lacy effect.

Requires a multiple of 4 sts.

Round 1: * P1, yo, ssk, P1, * repeat from * to * to end.
Round 2: * P2, K1, P1, * repeat from * to * to end.
Round 3: * P1, K2tog, yo, P1, * repeat from * to * to end.
Round 4: * P1, K1, P2, * repeat from * to * to end.

Repeat these 4 rounds.

2 Lacy Zigzag

Each yarn over is balanced by a corresponding decrease: see how "ssk" slopes to the left and "K2tog" slopes to the right.

Requires a multiple of 6 sts.

Round 1: * K1, yo, ssk, K3, * repeat from * to * to end.
Round 2: * K2, yo, ssk, K2, * repeat from * to * to end.
Round 3: * K3, yo, ssk, K1, * repeat from * to * to end.
Round 4: * K3, K2tog, yo, K1, * repeat from * to * to end.
Round 5: * K2, K2tog, yo, K2, * repeat from * to * to end.
Round 6: * K1, K2tog, yo, K3, * repeat from * to * to end.

Repeat these 6 rounds.

3 Old Shale

This traditional Shetland lace pattern is easy to work in circular knitting.

Requires a multiple of 12 sts.

Round 1: * [K2tog] twice, [yo, K1] 3 times, yo, [ssk] twice, K1 * repeat from * to * to end.
Round 2: P to end.

Repeat these 2 rounds.

TIPS

- Elongate Lace Zigzag pattern by alternating the given rounds with rounds of knit stitches.
- Try Old Shale pattern in stripes of different colors.

4 Lace Vees

A simple arrangement of yarn overs and decreases makes a pattern of lacy V-shapes.

Requires a multiple of 8 sts.

Round 1: * K4, yo, ssk, K2, * repeat from * to * to end.

Rounds 2, 4, 6, & 8: K to end.

Round 3: * K2, K2tog, yo, K1, yo, ssk, K1, * repeat from * to * to end.

Round 5: * K1, K2tog, yo, K3, yo, ssk, * repeat from * to * to end.

Round 7: * K2tog, yo, K6, * repeat from * to * to end.

Repeat these 8 rounds.

5 Tiny Flowers

Adding a small bobble to a lacy V-shape makes a tiny flower.

Requires a multiple of 10 sts.

Round 1: * K7, yo, ssk, K1, * repeat from * to * to end.

Rounds 2, 4, 6, 8, 10, & 12: K to end.

Round 3: * K5, K2tog, yo, K1, yo, ssk, * repeat from * to * to end.

Round 5: * K7, MSB, K2, * repeat from * to * to end.

Round 7: * K2, yo, ssk, K6, * repeat from * to * to end.

Round 9: * K2tog, yo, K1, yo, ssk, K5, * repeat from * to * to end.

Round 11: * K2, MSB, K7, * repeat from * to * to end.

Repeat these 12 rounds.

6 Lace Heart

Lace stitches can also be arranged to form simple motifs. Place this heart anywhere you like on your project.

Place 2 stitch markers 11 stitches apart and work the stitches between the markers as follows:

Round 1: K4, K2tog, yo, K5.

Rounds 2, 4, 6, 8, & 10: K11.

Round 3: K3, K2tog, yo, K1, yo, ssk, K3.

Round 5: K2, K2tog, yo, K3, yo, ssk, K2.

Round 7: K1, K2tog, yo, K5, yo, ssk, K1.

Round 9: K2tog, yo, K2, K2tog, yo, K3, yo, ssk.

Round 11: K2, [yo, S2togk, yo, K1] twice, K1.

Special Abbreviation

MSB = make small bobble (see page 73).

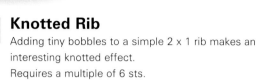

1 Knotted Rib

Adding tiny bobbles to a simple 2 x 1 rib makes an interesting knotted effect.

Requires a multiple of 6 sts.

Round 1: * P2, MSB, P2, K1, * repeat from * to * to end.

Rounds 2–4: * P2, K1, * repeat from * to * to end.

Round 5: * P2, K1, P2, MSB, * repeat from * to * to end.

Rounds 6–8: Repeat round 2.

Repeat these 8 rounds.

---

2 Daisy Stitch

This all-over pattern of raised bobbles can be used as a substitute for stockinette stitch.

Requires a multiple of 6 sts.

Round 1 & 2: K to end.

Rounds 3: * K3, PB, * repeat from * to * to end.

Round 4 & 5: K to end.

Rounds 6: * PB, K3, * repeat from * to * to end.

Repeat these 6 rounds.

---

3 Bobble and Block Stitch

Here, the small bobble adds interest to a simple checkerboard pattern.

Requires a multiple of 10 sts.

Rounds 1, 2, & 3: * K5, P5, * repeat from * to * to end.

Round 4: * K2, MSB, K2, P5, * repeat from * to * to end.

Rounds 5 & 6: Repeat round 1, twice.

Rounds 7, 8, & 9: * P5, K5, * repeat from * to * to end.

Round 10: * P5, K2, MSB, K2, * repeat from * to * to end.

Rounds 11 & 12: Repeat round 7, twice.

Repeat these 12 rounds.

Special Abbreviations

MSB = make small bobble (page 73)

PB = purl bobble (page 73)

MT = make tail: Using simple thumb cast-on (page 23), cast on 5 sts onto left needle tip, then bind off these 5 sts, leaving next (6th) st on right needle

4 Trinity Stitch

This classic stitch makes a crunchy, all-over texture.

Requires a multiple of 4 sts.

Round 1: P to end.

Round 2: * [P1, K1, P1] all into same st, K3tog, * repeat from * to * to end.

Round 3: P to end.

Round 4: * K3tog, [P1, K1, P1] all into same st, * repeat from * to * to end.

Repeat these 4 rounds.

5 Little Tails

These little tails are very easy to work, adding a bold texture to stockinette stitch.

Requires a multiple of 6 sts.

Rounds 1 & 2: K to end.

Round 3: * K5, MT, * repeat from * to * to end.

Rounds 4 & 5: K to end.

Round 6: * K2, MT, K3, * repeat from * to * to end.

Repeat these 6 rounds.

6 Leaf Border

These little leaves are worked on a background of reverse stockinette stitch (page 106). Begin with a multiple of 6 sts. The total stitch count varies from round to round.

Round 1: * P2, K1, P3, * repeat from * to * to end.

Round 2: * P2, m1tbl, K1, m1tbl, P3, * repeat from * to * to end.

Round 3: * P2, [K1, yo] twice, K1, P3, * repeat from * to * to end.

Round 4: * P2, K2, yo, K1, yo, K2, P3, * repeat from * to * to end.

Rounds 5 & 6: * P2, K7, P3, * repeat from * to * to end.

Round 7: * P2, K2tog, K3, ssk, P3, * repeat from * to * to end.

Round 8: * P2, K2tog, K1, ssk, P3, * repeat from * to * to end.

Round 9: *P2, S2togk, P3, * repeat from * to * to end.

Continue in reverse stockinette stitch.

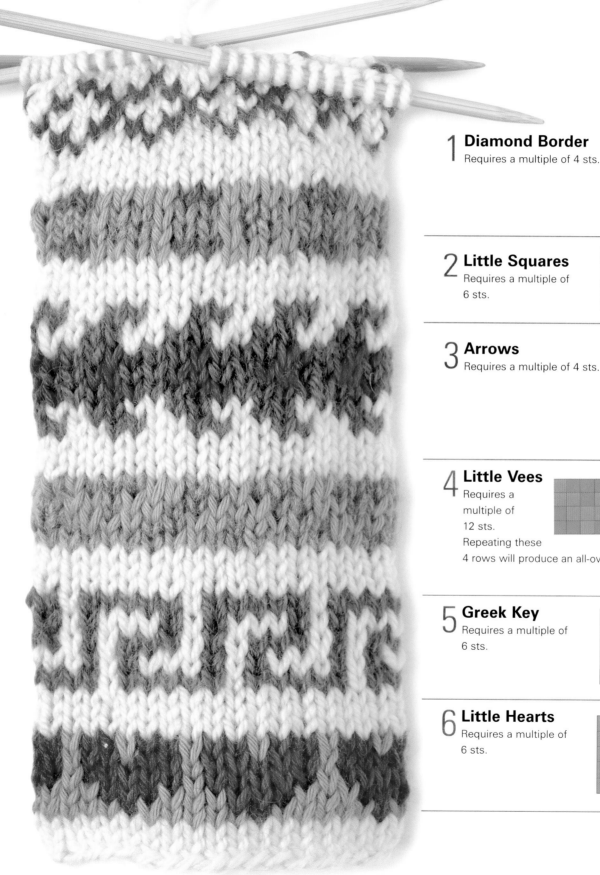

1 Diamond Border
Requires a multiple of 4 sts.

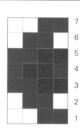

2 Little Squares
Requires a multiple of 6 sts.

3 Arrows
Requires a multiple of 4 sts.

4 Little Vees
Requires a multiple of 12 sts. Repeating these 4 rows will produce an all-over pattern of diamonds.

5 Greek Key
Requires a multiple of 6 sts.

6 Little Hearts
Requires a multiple of 6 sts.

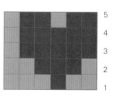

7 Large Hearts

Requires a multiple of 10 sts.

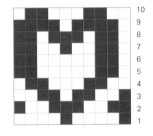

8 Flowers

Requires a multiple of 10 sts.

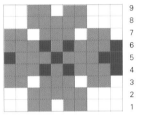

9 Snowflakes

Requires a multiple of 10 sts.

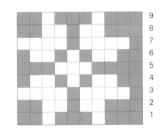

TIPS

- All the patterns on this page and opposite may be worked by the stranding method shown on page 82.
- Try combining bands of small and large fairisle patterns together in the same project.
- Plan your own designs with squared paper and colored pencils.

1 Spiral Lines

Use one ball of main color (color A) and several small balls of color B, one for each line.

The version shown requires a multiple of 12 sts, but you can adjust the spacing of the lines to suit your project.

Round 1: Read chart row 1 from right to left: * Join in a small ball of color B, K2, change to color A, K10, * repeat from * to * to end.

Continue reading subsequent rounds from chart, beginning at chart row 2.

Repeat these 12 rounds.

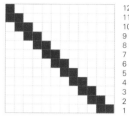

2 Zigzag Lines

Use a separate small ball of color B for each line and just one ball of main color (color A).

The version shown requires a multiple of 9 sts, but you can adjust the spacing of the lines to suit your project.

Round 1: Read chart row 1 from right to left: * Join in a small ball of color B, K2, change to color A, K7, * repeat from * to * to end.

Continue reading subsequent rounds from chart, beginning at chart row 2.

Repeat these 14 rounds.

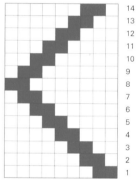

TIPS

- The technique for working these stitch patterns is shown on page 83.
- Remember, in circular knitting the right side of the work is always facing you, so all chart rows are read from right to left.
- Try working these traveling line patterns on a striped background.

3 Horizontal Zigzag

Use a separate length of color B for each chart repeat and just one ball of main color (color A). Requires a multiple of 12 sts.

Round 1: Read chart row 1 from right to left: * In color A, K6, K1 using center of a length of color B, change to color A, K5 * repeat from * to * to end. Continue reading subsequent rounds from chart, beginning at chart row 2, using one tail of color B for sts traveling left, and the other tail for sts traveling right.

Repeat these 14 rounds.

4 Diamond Trellis

Note that all the lines in color B travel to the left, and all those in color C travel to the right. Requires a multiple of 10 sts.

Round 1: Read chart row 1 from right to left: * Join in a ball of color B, K1, change to color A, K8, join in a ball of color C, K1, * repeat from * to * to end.

Continue reading subsequent rounds from chart, beginning at chart row 2.

Repeat these 10 rounds.

Resources

Yarn Suppliers

Four Seasons Knitting Products
89 Sarah Ashbridge Avenue
Toronto
ON M4L 3Y1
Canada
416–693–6848
www.fourseasonsknitting.com

King Cole
Merrie Mills
Elliot St, Keighley
W. Yorkshire BD20 ODE
UK
+44 (0)1535 650230
www.kingcole.co.uk

Knitting Fever Inc. and Euro Yarns
Roosevelt
NJ 11575
(516)–546–3600
www.knittingfever.com
(distributors of Debbie Bliss yarns)

Patons
320 Livingstone Avenue South
Listowel
ON N4W 3H3
1–888–368–8401
www.patonsyarns.com

Rowan USA
4 Townsend West, Suite 8
Nashua
NH 03063
603–886–5041
www.knitrowan.com

Unique Kolours
28 N. Bacton Hill Road
Malvern
PA 19355
610–644–4885
uniquekolours.com
(distributors of Colinette yarns)

Selected Retail Outlets

Changing Threads
326 Third Ave
Skagway
AK 99840
907–983–3700
www.changingthreads.com

Diamond Yarn
155 Martin Ross, Unit 3
Toronto
ON M3J 2L9
416–736–6111
www.diamondyarns.com

Fine Points
12620 Larchmere Blvd
Cleveland
OH 44120
216–229–6644
www.finepoints.com

Grace Robinson and Company
208 U.S. Route One
Freeport
ME 04032
207–865–6110
www.yarnandneedlepoint.com

Heidi's Yarnhaus
3966-B Airport Blvd
Pinebrook Center
Mobile
AL 36609
251–342–0088
www.yarnhaus.com

Jessica Knits
10401 E. McDowell
Mountain Ranch Rd #7
Scottsdale
AZ 85255
480–515–4454
www.jessicaknits.com

Jimmy Beans Wool
5000 Smithridge Drive #A11
Reno
NV 89502
775–827–9276
www.jimmybeanswool.com

Juniper Fiberworks
143 SW Century Drive Suite B
Bend
OR 97702
541–318–0726
www.juniperfiberworks.com

Knitter's Dream
2340 Mockingbird Road
Harrisburg
PA 17112
717–599–7665
www.knittersdream.com

Knitting Basket
5812 Grove Avenue
Richmond
VA 23226
804–282–2909
www.theknittingbasket.biz

Knitting Sisters
1915 B-1 Pocahontas Trail
Williamsburg
VA 23185
757–258–5005
www.knittingsisters.com

Knit2purl2
Newark
DE 19711
302–737–4917
www.knit2purl2.com

Lamb's Ear
4631 Pacific Ave
Tacoma
WA 98408
253–472–7695
www.lambsearfarm.com

Personal Threads
8025 West Dodge Road
Omaha
NE 68114–3413
402–391–7288
www.personalthreads.com

Purl
137 Sullivan Street
New York
NY 10012
212–420–8796
www.purlsoho.com

The Elegant Ewe
71 South Main Street
Concord
NH 03301
603–226–0066
www.elegantewe.com

The Needle Emporium
420 Wilson Street East
Ancaster
ON L9G 2C3
Canada
905–648–1994
www.needleemporium.com

The Yarn Boutique
357C Mt Diablo Blvd
Lafayette
CA 94549
925–283–7377
www.yarnboutique.us

The Yarn Nook
1261 Smoky Park Hwy
Candler
NC 28715
337–783–5565
www.yarnnook.com

The Yarn Shop
120 Bent Street, Suite B
Taos
NM 87571
505–758–9341
www.taosyarnshop.com

The Wool Connection
34 East Main Street
Old Avon Village N
Avon
CT 06001
860–678–1710
www.woolconnection.com

Wildflower Yarns And Knitwear
300 Poyntz Avenue
Manhattan
KS 66502
785–537–1826
www.wildflowerknits.com

Wool and Company
23 South Third Street
Geneva
IL 60134
630–232–2305
www.woolandcompany.com

Wool Trends
238 Hamilton Avenue
St John's
Newfoundland A1E 1J7
Canada
709–726–3242
www.wooltrends.ca

Wooly Monmouth
9 Monmouth Street
Red Bank
NJ 07701
732–224–YARN
www.woolymonmouth.com

WoolWinders
404 King Farm Boulevard
Rockville
MD 20850
240–632–YARN (9276)
www.woolwinders.com

Yarn Expressions
8415 Whitesburg Drive
Huntsville
AL
256–881–0260
www.yarnexpressions.com

Yarns Down Under
37C Hillside Terrace
Deep River
CT 06417
860–526–9986
www.yarnsdownunder.com

Yarn Lady
24371 Avenida de la Carlota
Suite M1 & 2
Oakbrook village
Laguna Hills
CA
949–770–7809
www.yarnlady.com

Index

Credits

The author would like to thank Claire Rowan, who knitted the samples for the Stitch Library, and also Brenda Lee Devantier—a very patient hand model.

Quarto would like to thank Abbie Horne at Mustard Models, Emma Sigurdsson, and baby Otto.